Lundy

A CHARGE TO KEEP:

RE-MISSIONING THE URBAN CHURCH FOR THE 21ST CENTURY

By Tokunbo Adelekan

A Publication of
*Progressive National Baptist Convention, Inc.
Congress Of Christian Education*

WHAT PEOPLE ARE SAYING ABOUT
A CHARGE TO KEEP

"In this book, **A Charge to Keep**, Tokunbo Adelekan looks at the interplay between sociology and salvation in explaining the deeply strained relations within North American congregations, conventions, and denominations. The methods of biblical appropriation, theological ethics, cultural interpretation, and sociological studies are used to unravel these difficulties and challenges. Adelekan is an emerging scholar in congregational and urban studies, attempting to delay some of the deep rifts across generations and cultures in our world today. Our cities, says Adelekan, may be on the return, but it is only possible if we bridge a gap between the cultural elites and those on the underside. This book is a must-read for those who seek the return of the American forces. It is a useful benchmark from which to look back and forward on the urban Church. The Bible tells us to write the vision and make it plain, and Adelekan's profound insights will help us to do so and to build dialogue on urban ministry for years to come."

—***Rev. Kip Banks,*** Interim General Secretary
Progressive National Baptist Convention, Inc.

"**A Charge to Keep** is a cross-cultural, trans-generational Christian manifesto and a must-read for those committed to congregational renewal and the liberation of people everywhere. It is written with clarity and brilliance born from the synthesis of academy and Church, the family and the faith, so wonderfully embodied in the person of Reverend Dr. Tokunbo Adelekan—Pastor, Professor and Prophet of our times."

—***Lawrence T. Foster,*** Senior Pastor
Calvary Baptist Church of Detroit, Michigan

"If one is looking for a book that will challenge the dichotomy between the Church and community, one need look no farther. **A Charge to Keep**, theologically and practically, assists its reader in understanding the Church's role both inside and outside its four walls. As a seasoned pastor and academician, I am confident that this book will enhance the ministry and lives of pastors, laypersons, professors, seminarians, community leaders, and social activists across denominational, geographical, sociological, and cultural lines. The breadth of Adelekan's scholarship and pastoral experience separates this book from other similar resources. The weaving of biblical, theological, and practical thought make it a credible resource for those longing for Church and community renewal."

> —*Wayne E. Croft, Sr., D.Min., Ph.D.*
> Senior Pastor, St. Paul's Baptist Church, West Chester, PA
> Jeremiah A. Wright, Sr. Associate Professor of Homiletics and Liturgics, Lutheran Theological Seminary at Philadelphia

"Jesus began his public ministry by announcing the arrival of the Kingdom of God. His ministry inaugurated a new reign of human flourishing and presentation of the Gospel. **A Charge to Keep** keeps this Christological focus by outlining the extraordinary hope that urban mission organizations can offer to our nation's high octane urban centers, teeming with people and change. This book is an invaluable resource for all seeking viable solutions to the problems of our cities and ways to contribute to discussion on the role of "faith-based organizations" and social policy. This book is exemplary in its claim that the progressive Christian is critical to the program to rehabilitate our nation's cities and must have a prophetic witness at its core. As a scholar who pastors a progressive urban Church, Adelekan has led his congregants to reclaim a lost part of their spirituality and community by launching a vigorous struggle to reclaim their missional identity and recover their inner city neighborhoods, family by family. He has done this not only by reaching out but also by building a strong sense of community, the necessary moral foundation without which the best-intentioned plans of government are sure to fail. Truly inspirational, refreshingly passionate and astoundingly timely, your sense of mission is bound to grow with the pages of this highly relevant work."

> —*Peter Hwang*
> First Korean Baptist Church Philadelphia, Inc.
> President, Korean Council, Southern Baptist Churches

"This book is a gift to the present and future Church. It provides a roadmap that every pastor, preacher, minister, and Church worker should follow. It is a message to so many dysfunctional Churches today. If this book is read and followed, the Church of tomorrow will be the Church that the Lord Jesus Christ left us in charge of. The Church has suffered in the past because of the lack of intellectual leadership that this book pursues. Tokunbo Adelekan, one of the leading scholar-preachers of his generation, has created a masterpiece that challenges the soul of the present day Church. It is a must-read by students in seminary, pastors, faith leaders, and all those who want to follow Jesus' teaching. It should be a must-read for anyone who seeks to teach in college, universities and seminaries. Adelekan has given us a way forward. It is a gift that we can't afford to pass up."

>—*W. Wilson Goode, Sr., D.Min.*
>President and CEO, Amachi, Inc.

"This book is full of "High Impact Action for God's Kingdom Business." It illustrates the urgency of the urban believer to address the pressing social ills facing family structure, schools, Churches, businesses, and the communities at large. It is a call for action on "spiritual awakening, regeneration and resurrection for all." An excellent resource for educators, Church workers, and policymakers."

>—*Michael Bentil, DBA*
>Associate Professor, Accounting & Finance
>Peirce College, Philadelphia, PA

"Reverend Tokunbo Adelekan demonstrated in his book, African Wisdom: 101 Proverbs from the Motherland, that he is spiritual and intellectual. He has a profound concern for the community. Adelekan, with intense thought, takes on the command from our Savior to "go ye therefore." In this book, **A Charge to Keep**, he takes on the topic of urban ministry. Many Christians say NO to urban ministry, explaining it is too dangerous, or we cannot meet the needs of the people. I agree with Adelekan; we do not get to choose who gets the Good News. I urge you to read this book and stop saying "NO" when God says "GO!"

>—*Pastor Albert Morgan*, "The Mailman"
>Senior Pastor, Union Baptist Temple, Bridgeton, NJ

"Dr. Tokunbo Adelekan's **A Charge to Keep** is an outstanding contribution to Christian thought and witness. His thorough assessment of Church life made from a deeply spiritual perspective engages many of the most sensitive issues of our day by using a biblical foundation, theological reflection, and experiences gathered through his work as a senior pastor and professor. Written in a sophisticated yet accessible style, **A Charge to Keep** calls pulpit and pew to become passionate instruments of God to transform a society poignantly plagued with social ills and religious conformity. Those who read this work will be intellectually stimulated, spiritually elevated, and persuaded to heed Dr. Adelekan's call to reshape American Christianity into a potent, enlightened, effective, empowering force rightfully taking her place as earth's salt and light."

> **—Edward L. Taylor**
> Royal Holloway College, The University of London, UK
> Editor, The Words of Gardner Taylor

"Dr. Adelekan has harnessed the critical thinking of a scholar with the sensitivity of a shepherd to address the plight of the urban Church. He outlines the organizational structure, programmatic thrust, and leadership of the urban Church, which has created, not kingdom advancement, but spiritual inertia resulting in congregational malaise, financial lockjaw, and shrinking membership. Professor Adelekan challenges the Church and its leadership to find answers to this dilemma by revisiting the early Church whose only resource was the Gospel of Jesus Christ, coupled with the power of the Holy Spirit. If you are a pastor, Church leader, seminarian, or teacher who is challenged by this concern, then **A Charge To Keep** is a resource that will not only stimulate self-reflection, but also provide some refreshing anecdotes accomplished through the transformative power of the Holy Spirit."

> **—Warren H. Marshall, Jr.**
> Pastor, North Penn Baptist Church
> Chairman, Property and Finance
> Progressive National Baptist Convention

"Written from a place of passion and humility, this book is like a mini-spiritual retreat for the reader who reads reflectively. **A Charge to Keep** combines theology and biblically based principles and responds to the reality of the urban context with integrity. It invites us to congruency between the spoken word and the incarnate message of the Church. Written with clarity and depth, the author's message is for the pastoral and congregational leadership. If we take it seriously, it can lead us towards a revival."

> **—Elizabeth Conde-Frazier, MDiv., PhD.**
> Dean and Vice President of Education at Esperanza College of Eastern University, St. Davids, PA

A CHARGE TO KEEP

RE-MISSIONING THE URBAN CHURCH
FOR THE 21ST CENTURY

TOKUNBO ADELEKAN

A Charge To Keep: Re-Missioning The
Urban Church For The 21st Century

©2014 Tokunbo Adelekan

ISBN (13) 978-1-93977-14-9

Published by MMGI Books
Chicago, Illinois
www.mmgibooks.com

Cover and Interior Design by LaTanya Orr
Selah Branding & Design, LLC • www.iselah.com

Cover Art/Illustration by Peter Pagast & Jane Golden,
Peace Wall | Mural Arts Program, Philadelphia, PA
http://muralarts.org/collections/projects/peace-wall

Photo of Peace Wall by Jack Ramsdale

All rights reserved, including the right of reproduction in whole or in part in any form. No part of this book may be reproduced by any mechanical, photographic or electronic process without expressed written permission from the author.

Printed in the United States of America.

TABLE OF CONTENTS

ACKNOWLEDGEMENTS   *xi*

FOREWORD
Dr. Johnny Ray Youngblood   *xiii*

PROLOGUE
Dr. Harold Dean Trulear   *xvii*

PREFACE   *xix*

INTRODUCTION: The Testimony of a Tree   *xxvii*

PART ONE: SETTING THE HOUSE IN ORDER   1

    1. For This Cause: Ecclesial Foundations   3

    2. I Shall Give You Shepherds:
       Pastoral Care and Prayer   15

    3. Ye Shall Receive Power: The Holy Spirit
       and the Church as Community of Compassion   29

    4. Making It Plain: The Vision Imperative   41

    5. Not By Power, Nor By Might: Spiritual Warfare
       and Compassion   51

**PART TWO: THE DAMASCUS ENCOUNTER:
IN SEARCH OF THE GODLY CITY**   69

    6. A Hole in My Soul: Nihilism and the Church   73

    7. Killing Me Softly: The Gods of Mammon   85

    8. God Bless the Child That's Got His Own:
       Rising Debt and Income Inequality   103

9. Big Money and the New "Jim Crow" — 117

10. Quilting Hope: The Changing Face of Parenting and Families — 137

11. Sankofa: The Blessings and Burdens of Urban Education in America — 151

CONCLUSION: TO SERVE THIS PRESENT AGE: THE CHURCH LIVING IN THE SPIRIT — 167

EPILOGUE — 171

SELECT BIBLIOGRAPHY — 177

ACKNOWLEDGEMENTS

This work is made possible—as is all my work—by my loving family: Tahira, Adeola, Adedotun, and Adebayo. Apart from the efforts of my family, the success of any project depends largely on the encouragement and guidance of many others. I take this opportunity to express my gratitude to the people who have been instrumental in the successful completion of this project. I would like to show my greatest appreciation to The Congress of Christian Education of the Progressive National Baptist Convention, especially Lamont Duane Brown, vice president at large; Priscilla Loney, chairman; and James Evans, vice chairman. Without their enabling patience and humble guidance, this essay would never have seen the light of day. At Palmer Theological Seminary the encouraging support of Dr. Loida Martell-Otero provided much-needed balm in the process. I can't say enough about her tremendous support and help. I don't think I would have finished this work without her angelic nudging. Much appreciation to former students and present ministerial assistants Andre Price, Cheryl Hargrave, Tiffany Murphy, and Stephanie Wilson-Benson (all products of Palmer Theological Seminary) for their consistent contribution to the development of the work. I feel motivated and encouraged every time I walk onto Palmer's campus. Very special thanks to Jeron Frame, a woman of tremendous grace and vision, who read through and engaged with the entire manuscript. In addition, without the careful attentiveness of Ulrike Guthrie this essay would not have materialized. The guidance and support received from all the members who contributed and who are contributing to this project was vital for its success. I am grateful for their constant support and help. Thanks to J. Nicole Morgan for research help and for encouragement, reflective insights, and countless points, and for editing significant portions of the essay. I am also grateful for the invaluable encouragement from my colleagues Willette A. Burgie-Bryant, Marsha Brown Woodard, and George Hancock-Stefan.

A deeply felt thank you to Wayne Croft, Lawrence Foster, Elizabeth Conde-Frazier, Cassandra Hill, Peter Hwang, L. B. Jones, Charles McNeil, Ed Taylor, Britt Starghill, Albert Morgan, Jr., Warren Marshall, Damone Jones, and Donald Dunnigan for their invaluable contributions and for friendship that goes well beyond the call of duty.

To two persons above all others—except my wife—I owe incommensurable debts: Johnny Ray Youngblood and Clarence James. Their enabling teaching and invaluable coaching have indelibly shaped my thinking and writing.

Others to whom I owe prioritized debts of gratitude are the Philadelphia Baptist Association (PBA), the Pennsylvania Eastern Keystone Baptist Association, and the Bethany Baptist Association for sharing their institutional resources in ways that greatly informed my understanding of urban ministry.

I am grateful to all my friends and co-workers in ministry from Mount Olivet Tabernacle Baptist Church: Ethel Ellis, Bessie Session, Alverita Spain, Joseph Jenkins, Carel Floyd, Jo Walker, Helen Hill, Doc Godwin, William Dillard, Lois Owens, and Vikki Leach. To the brilliant flock of Mount Olivet Tabernacle Baptist, the "Church on Purpose," and my overwhelming heartfelt source of pastoral contentment: much gratitude for all their encouragement that this book would help the real work of transformation that is much needed in so many urban centers and cities across America.

FOREWORD

By Dr. Johnny Ray Youngblood

Dr. Adelekan's pronouncement in these pages is like a diamond scratching the reigning mirror veneer of this present-day Church. This "penmanship call" seeks to "transform" the crafted structure of Church today into a resurrected entity that truly evidences the power/personality of our founder and chief, Jesus of Nazareth.

I am grateful that Dr. Adelekan views the condition of the Church and community from the coin of vantage of both the pastor to a local congregation and professor to promising and engaged Church leaders.

This work, led of the Holy Ghost, has been borne again up out of the crucible of pastoral pain. This, along with the witness of scripture, is the authority that backs and bolsters this epistle of a call/recall to the body of Christ.

Dr. Adelekan, interestingly enough, accents in this written call the must, the indispensable need for a healthy Church. He appears in this work to be a caring physician at the bedside of his patient, reading all of the vital signs and diagnoses. Yet, in an unmistakable posture of hope, ministers even while the patient is on life support refusing to consent to DNR approval. Until the patient flatlines, look for improvement, and if such occurs, he is prepared in a most capable fashion to engage the heart-jolting paddles of scripture to resuscitate believing in the eternality of the ecclesia. The "another comforter" to the world.

And how refreshing and surprisingly provocative to have a scholar of the day to connect the dots of doctrine and center his outline in and around the Holy Ghost. *A Charge to Keep* is to me a fountain of hope. Like *Your God Is Too Small* by J.B. Phillips, one reading is just not enough. In kinship to the scriptures; it is "unfathomable." This work should be a must-read for all seminary personnel and active pastors who yet read and those believers, both lay and clergy, who know that writing is one of the ordained ministries of the Church. God yet speaks through books.

In conclusion, Dr. Adelekan speaks passionately of and to the local Church. It is my prayer that this work will be picked up and would penetrate the denominational judicatories of the Church as well. Let them that have ears, Hear!

A charge to keep I have,
a God to glorify,
a never-dying soul to save,
and fit it for the sky.

To serve the present age,
my calling to fulfill;
O may it all my powers engage
to do my Master's will!

Charles Wesley

PROLOGUE

By Dr. Harold Dean Trulear, Ph.D.
Associate Professor of Applied Theology
Howard University School of Divinity
Washington, D.C.

With contemporary theological texts—systematic, liberationist, and applied—focusing on relevance and contemporary change, Dr. Adelekan's work here provides a simple yet sophisticated call back to basics. A biblically based, theologically researched, and experientially lived project, this book reminds us of the basis of what it means to be Church. It also calls Church leadership, both present and future, to a reckoning of standard, and not captive to popular issues, no matter how just the cause.

Adelekan's call back to a biblical and theological basis for ekklesia challenges Churches to examine the ground of their being, their divine raison d'être. As I pen this forward, for example, I am in Iowa to train congregations on how to deal with mass incarceration. My national work in this area, under the rubric "Healing Communities," makes the important point that congregations should be involved in the social justice issue of disproportionate Black confinement in the criminal justice system.

But Adelekan's text offers a caution to "specialized ministries" such as my own. I would put it this way: No one ever said, "There are too many Black people in jail. Let's start a Church." Rather, by pointing to the essentials of ecclesiology, Adelekan argues that the reasons for being Church transcend contemporary issues of justice and are grounded in what he clearly defines as purpose. And the issues we face, whether mass incarceration, family disintegration, poverty, or anything else, do not determine the purpose of the Church. Rather, by focusing on the purpose to which God called, Jesus established, and the Spirit empowered, the Church should lead through a process of discernment by which congregations, out of their praise, prayer, and preaching, discover ministries both priestly and prophetic that flow from the basics. Therefore, people like me in specialized ministries must join with the discernment process of the ekklesia in order to be true to the Gospel.

Indeed, Adelekan diplomatically challenges all Church leaders with a litmus test centered on faithfulness to issues by asking whether or not we are faithful to essentials, whether or not our commitment is to issues, and whether or not Jesus is an appropriate leveraging mechanism to achieving our personal commitments to issues, no matter how just they may be.

This is a text that reflects upon and challenges us all to the practice of theological integrity and Christian discernment. All of us know people who have joined Churches because that congregation fits their political ideology, whether right or left. Adelekan argues for a normative ecclesiology out of which the process of a Spirit-led discernment determines the direction of ministry.

PREFACE

Several years ago I remember praying fervently for God to fund the non-profit organizations I was serving. We sorely needed financial resources to advance our work of training ministers, empowering lay leaders, and enabling teens in the tri-state area of Pennsylvania, New Jersey, and Delaware. I will never forget the aggressive shaking that the Comforter and Counselor, the Holy Spirit, gave me. The Spirit said, "Brother Tokunbo, don't pray for resources. Pray for relationships, and when you bless and honor the relationships that I give you, I will make sure that you and your organization will never lack for anything."

The Holy Spirit made His point. Building relationships is the priority. People are the spiritual leader's greatest resources, just as people are God's greatest resources. Christ came to bring us into relationship with God, and nothing should be more important to the spiritual leader than to bring people into the promises that God has for their lives.

BUILD RELATIONSHIPS THROUGH REVELATION: THE EXAMPLE OF JOSEPH

Wisdom is about tapping into God's promises. It is about discerning God's intentions for our lives. The life of Joseph is a gallant example of a life lived according to the will of God. His ability to interpret God's will brings him into Pharaoh's palace. In interpreting Pharaoh's dreams, the young man from Hebron establishes that God is the author and arranger of the dream. God has disclosed to Pharaoh what He intends to do for Egypt. In an unexpected and rare moment of royal transparency, Pharaoh also indicates that Joseph's wisdom comes from God. The self-disclosure of God to Joseph and Pharaoh unites both men in a classic partnership of power and purpose. They form a covenant based on mutual God-consciousness. Both men know they need each other and that they need God. When God moves to establish something eternal on earth, God creates a team, not for individuals' mutual aggrandizement or self-promotion, but for the benefit of others. Work that flows out of love and grace establishes the kingdom of righteousness. Selflessness, stewardship, and servanthood mark such work.

God used the balance of humility, integrity, and ability embodied by these two unusual personages to enable an entire nation for many years to come. This is God's way. God builds relationships so that other relationships can be nourished, protected, and preserved. Relationships with others flow from our relationship with God. Only in relationship with God do we develop the right spiritual disciplines, emotional patterns, thought commitments, and social habits to lead lives of spiritual flourishing. We cannot develop the ability to lead God's people without the mind of God. "For the vision is yet for an appointed time, but at the end it shall speak, and not lie; though it tarry, wait for it; because it will surely come" (Hab. 2:3). In the Gospel of John, Jesus says to his disciples:

> *Abide in me as I abide in you. Just as the branch cannot bear much fruit by itself unless it abides in the vine, neither can you unless you abide in me. I am the vine, you are the branches. Those who abide in me and I in them bear much fruit, because apart from me you can do nothing (John 15:4-5).*

"Apart from me you can do nothing." To lead without Christ is to love without a heart, to breathe without oxygen. The divine imprimatur is of utmost importance. All human leaders have frailties, foibles, and failures. Those who exercise credible servant leadership over time are those who have a heart to know God, a heart developed over years of discipline and sacrifice. The leader's capacity for self-control and emotional balance is the fruit of a transformed consciousness. Paul calls this the state of having a "renewed mind." Spiritual wisdom flows out from God to spiritually mature people. "Put on the new man who is renewed in knowledge according to the image of him who created him" (Col. 3:20). "Where there is no vision, the people perish" (Prov. 29:18).

In order to lead from the inside out and to empower the organization by empowering others, the leader must lead from a state of emotional health. To be emotionally healthy means to be in touch with one's faults and to use those as a gracious lens through which to view the flaws of others. Strength, vigor, and insight come through the healing of oneself. It is this process that forges deeper dependency on God's will and God's way. In this way our wounds, not just our gifts and talents, become sanctified.

Such healing from brokenness often leads to humility, and this attracts others to the leader's vision. John the Baptist's "I must decrease so he can increase" is a classic instantiation of this process. For N. Graham Standish, to empower others "takes a willingness to relinquish control and the need to have authority over others.

It takes a willingness to let others be responsible and to receive credit for the results of their own efforts." [1]

> *Leadership also takes practice, as Dave Martin reminds us:*
> *God wants us to think His thoughts about every situation that confronts us in our lives, and He wants us to think those thoughts "day and night." In other words, God wants us to read the Bible and gradually learn how He thinks so we can think like He thinks all the time. God knows the thoughts we think are destined to become habits in our behavior. He knows the thoughts we think are bound to become either life (which follows good thoughts) or death (which follows bad thoughts). So God wants us to retain our thinking by thinking correctly all the time so we can learn to focus our lives on things that will produce greatness for us.* [2]

Leaders who are not open to divine wisdom and not willing to develop good spiritual and leadership habits imperil their people, organizations, and communities. Shortsighted leadership can lead to organizational dysfunction, social collapse, economic decline, heightened crime rates, war, and even death on a large scale. As people of God, we are called to be wise servant leaders.

The true servant leader empowers others by focusing on aligning their gifts, talents, and experiences with the goals of the organization. This process of alignment requires trust. Those being led must be confident that the leader is making decisions that are in the best interests of the organization as a whole and of them as individuals.

Such leaders also develop the gift of encouragement. To encourage others means to infuse them with confidence and courage, happiness and hope. Because they are emotionally fragile, many

---

[1] N. Graham Standish, Becoming a Blessed Church (Herndon, VA: Alban Institute, 2005), 148.
[2] See "Learn How God Thinks – The Daily With Dr. Dave," June 7. davemartin.org/learn-god-thinks-daily-dr-dave-june-7/

people wrestle with doubt and despair. Because organizations are made up of people, they likewise wrestle with dysfunction. Typically when an organization is in decline, it first loses energy, then support, and then people. Eventually there is nothing left but a shell of the past. The main task of the Christian leader in times like these is to re-establish courage and trust in the organization, and that means instilling courage and trust in the individuals who invest in the organization's daily life. Trust is built and earned through partnering together on central matters of the faith: learning to love Christ and wholehearted, sacrificial service to others en route to personal betterment and an unfolding surrender to the Lord of creation. The holy triumvirate of the New Testament Gospel ministry we have come to adopt at Mount Olivet Tabernacle Baptist Church is "Worship, Word, and Work," as carried out through prayer, Bible reading, and stewardship.

Regular encouragement is particularly vital to combat the "accuser of the saints" found in every Christian community. This accuser tries to confuse the body of Christ and tempt believers with sin. Also known as the "adversary," his ultimate goal is to defame the Church and destroy its mission. Many modern Christians rationalize this demonic and destructive work of Satan as mere myth, as the stuff of primitive Christianity, as the result of human ignorance, psychic dysfunction, or cultural and social decay. Such attitudes do not address the weight and complexity of evil that creates such high levels of mayhem, misery, and madness. The empowering leader must become adept at recognizing the nature of evil and the cycles of violence that undermine and seek to destroy communities of faith. The leader can instead reshape the minds of believers, empowering them to utilize the word of God in all aspects of their lives. The empowering leader who leads out of love armed with truth helps guide his or her people from confusion into consciousness. The authentic leader knows that the source of his or her strength, compassion, vision, and quickening is the Spirit.

That leader habitually calls upon the Spirit for help in discernment and decision-making.

The empowering leader is a giver. This leader has developed a sacrificial ethic that flows out of his or her sense of calling and out of the awareness of the grace of God that orders all life (Psalm 1). Such a leader knows that God gives plentifully in order that we can in turn give generously. The Ndebele of Africa understand this paradox and say, "Giving is storing up for yourself." Time, talent, testimony, treasure, intelligence, presence, creativity, and imagination are all part of the package of self that the leader offers to others.

LEAD OTHERS TO LOVE

In many ways the life of Joseph prefigures Jesus the Christ. His enslavement and eventual vindication mirrors the crucifixion and resurrection of Jesus Christ. The empowering leader establishes his or her authenticity like Joseph and Jesus by building upon no other foundation than God. Dependence on God leads to appropriate spiritual influence. For though people may trust an ungodly leader for a season, eventually the organization will fizzle and die. God must first trust the leader; then God gives special spiritual influence to the leader to become a steward of His people. The leader then must positively support, educate, enable, and inform the people that he or she is blessed to lead. The results of trusting leadership are mindboggling: the Church takes on new life. People envision and pursue new possibilities. Nagging difficulties become sources of strengthening. Stumbling blocks become stepping-stones. Chaos turns into order and love. "The Peace Prayer," written by the sublime St. Francis of Assisi, exemplifies the relational elasticity and spiritual sobriety that buoys the missional audacity of such soulful servants of Christ:

Lord, make me an instrument of Thy peace;

Where there is hatred, let me sow love;

Where there is injury, pardon;

Where there is error, the truth;

Where there is doubt, the faith;

Where there is despair, hope;

Where there is darkness, light;

And where there is sadness, joy.

O Divine Master,

Grant that I may not so much seek

To be consoled, as to console;

To be understood, as to understand;

To be loved as to love.

For it is in giving that we receive;

It is in pardoning that we are pardoned;

And it is in dying that we are born to eternal life.

Amen.

INTRODUCTION

THE TESTIMONY OF A TREE

Beautiful is the moment in which we understand that we are no more than an instrument of God; we live only as long as God wants us to live; we can only do as much as God makes us able to do; we are only as intelligent as God would have us be.
　—Oscar A. Romero, The Violence of Love

The Church must be reminded that it is not the master or the servant of the state, but rather the conscience of the state. It must be the guide and the critic of the state, and never its tool. If the Church does not recapture its prophetic zeal, it will become an irrelevant social club without moral or spiritual authority.
　—Martin Luther King, Jr., Strength to Love

THE BAOBAB CHURCH

I could begin by expounding on the ills of society: poverty, consumerism, financial debt, sexual recklessness, unemployment, costly health care, decaying public school systems, weak family structures, and a general lack of trust of political authority. But you know all that. So instead of expounding on those realities, let me remind you instead of what the Church does well. And let me tell you by using the metaphor of the most wonderful tree.

The baobab tree (Adansonia digitata) is also known as "the tree of life." It is one of the most unusual trees on earth. Its branches resemble roots of other trees. Known for its resilience and resourcefulness, it lives in more than thirty countries across the globe. It has come to symbolize positivity, dignity, and adaptability. It provides food, shelter, and heat for the inhabitants of the savannah region of Africa. During the rainy season it stores up water and other valuable nourishment to use during the dry season when other plants wither and die. It is able to produce fruit under the most unfavorable conditions; hence its name, "the tree of life." All its parts can be used—for food, fiber, dye, and fuel.

Its resourcefulness is matched by its longevity. It has become a symbol of hope, longsuffering adaptability, and moral stamina. The "tree of life" is a universal symbol for God's shining faithfulness and unbreakable covenant in a struggling world. And for those who are stewards of this economy of grace, charged with the task of keeping their lanterns burning, the baobab tree is a symbol of spiritual resilience and radiance.

Amidst our urban dramas, Jesus calls us, His Church, to stand firm in its "baobabness": to remain unshaken amidst urban uncertainty, and to be capable, adaptable, flexible, courageous, and full of integrity. What is most exciting about the baobab-like Church is that its constancy allows it to adapt to external stimuli and by so doing transform its environment. It does this through three processes:

I. Internal cleansing (getting real with itself)
II. Adaptation to external stimuli (being relevant)
III. Transformation of its environment (being redemptive)

These steps may serve as a useful framework for the Church's work in urban America.

First, the Church is called to renew itself from the inside. By shedding what is unneeded it can remain healthy and faithful to its identity, which is a prerequisite for growth. I call this process "getting real with itself." The Church gets real by reminding itself of its founding purpose: to make mature disciples of Jesus Christ through loving worship of God and gracious service to neighbor. Secondly, because the internal cleansing process allows it to respond appropriately to stimuli, the Church is commissioned to respond constructively to what goes on around it and to bring life out of death. Thirdly, just as the baobab tree becomes a home to birds and animals that would otherwise perish without its nurturing presence and protective covering, so, too, the Church becomes the lifeline to those that would otherwise perish in the urban wasteland. Its protective and providing presence enables and empowers the less fortunate to have creative agency in the midst of hard and dehumanizing conditions. Like the baobab, all parts of the Church can be used to serve the human spirit. The Church has the wherewithal to remain vital despite enormous change and stress and to be a continuously renewed blessing to its community.

What does that blessing look like? Every day Christians gather to sing and pray and do their witness. Against innumerable odds and taxing circumstances, these persons and families witness that God can bring the impossible to fruition.

Take Shemah, for example. Shemah's father has cancer. Her parents are not currently married. Yet every weekday morning she wakes up at 4:30 to study and work. No one in her family has graduated from college, but Shemah is valedictorian of her high school class. Meet Helen. She is a single mother and grandmother. She is a Church trustee, spends time teaching Bible study, and reads passionately every day. She is a woman of great faith and indomitable courage, whose passion for mentoring and caring for the children in the neighborhood burns like a fire in her bones.

Carwell adores the "house of prayer." He serves his pastor with reckless abandon. Though he does not make a lot of money working several odd jobs during the week, he goes to great lengths to provide for his childhood sweetheart. When Carwell is not on a job, he exhausts himself caring for his physically challenged landlord. Additionally, he serves his Church by cleaning the building, working in the kitchen, and winning souls.

Finally, let me introduce you to Elijah, a tall strapping nineteen year old, who reads medical journals, writes plays, and will go to any length to pray for someone struggling with life's deepest problems. Raised by a single mother who is also a dynamic ordained minister, Elijah embodies the Socratic dictum, "the unexamined life is not worth living." One can only be drawn to his combination of critical intelligence, compassion, and charm, gifts that remind one of the quiet leadership of Oscar Romero, the intrepid compassion of Vernon Jordan, and the brilliant imagination of Maya Angelou.

Shema, Helen, Carwell, and Elijah are baobabs. They store up and use their resources to benefit those around them on behalf of Christ. They are witnesses to the vitality of their faith.

This book is about the Church's pastoral and prophetic witness. It is about theology in the trenches, about being baobabs in the city, about redeeming humanity, and healing the cultural and the moral decay that pervades communities, especially the crammed urban centers where the majority of the nation's poor live, love, and labor.

The health of the Church is critical for the health of the community that it inhabits. Church and community indwell each other. As the Church goes so does the community, perhaps especially in urban environments. Too many congregations are overwhelmed by systemic problems such as poor education, chronic poverty, relentless crime, neighborhood decline, cultural decadence, as well as emotional challenges such as indifference, anxiety, worry, hopelessness, and despair. These problems often fuse to create a culture of poverty within congregations that is characterized by a lack of vision and foresight, declining attendance, infighting, and ecclesiastical lethargy—in short, a culture that is unable to address the larger systemic issues that create social misery and forge oppressive circumstances. This book seeks to chart a way out of our present malaise, our valley of dry bones, a way out that is evidence of having been led by the Spirit of God into healthy Churches, people, and communities.

We as the Church are called by God to serve the poor and the oppressed. In many urban communities, the Church of Jesus Christ still occupies huge moral and political space. Unfortunately, congregations more often than not emphasize what happens during the "worship hour" when people and pastor, pulpit and pew are at their "Sunday best" and pay scant attention to the six days following Sunday. Yet it is precisely on those six days that we, the people of God, are called to live out the full meaning of our faith and bear witness to the love-ethic of Jesus Christ. When we do not live out our faith, we stagnate.

Leaders of urban congregations daily navigate the stresses and storms of urban life. They pay bills, repair and maintain buildings, run the nursery schools and soup kitchens, visit the sick, attend town meetings, consult community leaders, and develop their staff. And when these all-too-human needs are not met with vigor and integrity, Churches begin the slow but steady descent towards decay and death. I wonder how we can talk about liberation when the "Old Ship of Zion" leaks and is constantly on the verge of running aground? How are we to arrive in the Promise Land when the vehicle of freedom remains tied to Egyptian idols? How do we develop true ends when we have faulty means?

We must maintain our connection to the Holy Spirit. Maintaining "buildings and budgets" is a worthy task for the Church, but even without those tasks, the Spirit will still be at work. Yet that reality can be hard to believe if we're not reminded of it. One member of my Church discovered this truth:

> *Just this past winter, we have not been able to use our sanctuary for worship. Our pipes froze, causing breaks in the pipes, water damage and damage to our boiler. We haven't missed a service yet; we've been worshipping in our lower sanctuary for almost six months now. Our congregation has grown closer, our services have reached another level of worship—it just continues to get better and better. Our congregants are so much more open to the Holy Spirit than ever before.* [1]

The average urban parishioner is either out of work or overworked. More often than not she is single, female, and a mother or grandmother of working-class background, forced to make do under intolerable conditions. Wise Church administration must pay attention to the health of those who are already sitting in the pews as well as those groups that we seek to bring in as disciples and witnesses of the living God. Congregational health is key for the witness of the Church to the world.

Rev. Wyatt Tee Walker, one of the luminaries of the twentieth-century Black Church, often said that Black worship can be characterized by the three P's: praying, praising, and preaching. While this trilogy captures the experience of Sunday worship, and many books have

---

1 Email interview with Val, June 2014.

been written on the worthiness and dynamism of this experience, the worship triumvirate must be complemented by the triumvirate of planning, programming, and purpose-setting. The 21st century Church must make the latter trilogy foundational to the way it lives out the first trilogy.

The lack of structures of accountability and deficient Church administration mechanisms create organizational dysfunction that deadens enterprise, initiative, and hope. Who wants to worship in a setting besieged by rancor and divisiveness, caught in the generation trap, or held hostage by worship wars? Or among a people whose witness is humdrum and sanitized, devoid of missional imagination and generative courage? These are climates in which people are chronically unsure about their futures. Poor planning creates an anxiety that inhibits the spirit of connectedness that is central to worshipping together. Inefficiency is primarily due to mismanagement of time, lack of trust, undisciplined communities, a lack of understanding of (and appreciation for) the role of the pastor, unclear accountability structures, tension between senior ministers and boards, and the lukewarm commitment among members. Such inefficiency and lack of vitality weaken the collective witness of the people of God.

The message of the Church cannot be separated from its story in Christ. The Church's proclamation of this message must be distinguishable in all its practice. Our practice is preaching. Our lives and lifestyles present a particular message to a world hungry for answers that we claim can only be found in Christ. How we live in relationship to Christ is our most visible witness. How we embody Christ is critical to the world's reception of Him. Ideally, we show the world how to live by becoming a community of persons unified in Christ and living out the love-ethic that is at the heart of the Gospel. The Church is most thoroughly the Church when it stands in loving unity as one under the Lordship of Jesus Christ.

Before we relate to the community outside of the Church, we are first a community shaped by the truth that is Jesus Christ. Any message to the world must be rooted in our collected lives as being rooted in Christ. This is one important and foundational way that we build each other up in Jesus Christ. We express who and what the Church is by how we behave towards one another (Eph. 4:13; Heb. 10; 24:25; Rom. 14:1, 19). The more we allow ourselves to be influenced by Jesus and by the Holy Spirit, the more we are transformed into compelling ambassadors of Christ.

THE WAY OF CULTURE

Civil America is hemorrhaging at its core. The once formidable social norms of care and concern have either vanished from plain sight or are being displaced by an ethic of self-preservation. Ours is a culture of unabashed self-promotion, clannish thinking, and tribal solidarity. As a consequence, civility and accountability, which once seemed to be buzzwords of social status and the staples of middle-class America, sound old hat or even imprudent to many. This loss, one that has engendered a gaping disregard for authentic community, betrays the widespread confusion about the integrity and validity of traditional sources of meaning—political parties, social clubs, religious spaces, work places, even college campuses. As these spaces have become desacralized, American citizens have become disenchanted, disloyal, and self-centered. From city to country there is a gnawing cynicism that promises are made to be broken. Hence, public pronouncements by government officials or corporate representatives are experienced more as glib ideological sound bites or glitzy marketing tools rather than moral testimonies, as entertaining spoofs rather than a down payment on a healthy future. Civility is no longer in vogue. Integrity has become passé. The media is afire with scandal. A society drenched in paranoia, cynicism, and delusions of grandeur spawns a generation of victims who are incorrigibly distrustful—for good reason.

This all especially seems to be the case in urban America and the Christian Church. Daily we receive reports of a society under siege: abuse of power, the curtailment of beauty, the violation of human dignity, and the enshrinement of social recklessness is woven into the warp and woof of our daily expectation. We suffer from a lack of authentic relationships and companionship. As W.B. Yeats wrote in "*The Second Coming,*" [2]

> *Things fall apart; the centre cannot hold;*
> *Mere anarchy is loosed upon the world,*
> *The blood-dimmed tide is loosed, and everywhere*
> *The ceremony of innocence is drowned.*

We seem to care less and less about the increasing fragmentation and alienation that characterizes our common life. Howard Thurman taught that contact without community is a dangerous thing and that it creates the conditions for profound alienation and animosity in the human mind.[3] The Roman soldier and the Galilean Jewish peasant saw each other on a daily basis, but their loathing for each other was often consuming and incorrigible. It may be that this same feeling characterizes much of U. S. society today, especially in urban communities fraught with distractions and decay. The globe may be shrinking, economic barriers may have become less formidable, but this does not mean that we have a regard for the humanity of all those we see. If we do not come together as human beings it is quite likely that, as Dr. Martin Luther King taught, we will die separately as fools.

Urban America is bombarded by images of mayhem, war, and violence. Our desire to be loved is not satisfied; our need for

---

[2] Wm. B. Yeats, The Collected Poems (Hertfordshire, UK: Wordsworth Editions Ltd., 2000), 158.
[3] For a wonderful treatment of how draconian systems conspire to dehumanize the marginalized, see Howard Thurman's classic Jesus and the Disinherited (Boston: Beacon Press, 1976). Thurman gives affirmation and agency to those who routinely suffer the darts of depersonalization. Jesus provides a nonviolent method of moral agency that affirms deliverance without self-defeating behavior.

credible spaces of acceptance is not understood. Hence, many of our neighbors are losing their capacity to connect, to speak, to be heard. The feeling of "me against the world" masks the deep feeling of alienation that creates depression and psychological isolation. The ligatures that fostered community and gave us access to each other have been broken. We care less about each other because there is an increasing feeling that there is nothing to care for. We see that the cost of the lack of trust in society also seems to work against other forms of cooperation and injures our social cohesion and our economic health. I suggest that we need to return to our foundations in order to find our way through the City. Our pilgrimage on the Damascus road is bound to bring us into the path of our Lord—if we are faithful!

PART ONE

SETTING THE HOUSE IN ORDER

About that time Hezekiah became deathly ill, and the prophet Isaiah son of Amoz went to visit him. He gave the king this message: "This is what the LORD says: Set your affairs in order, for you are going to die. You will not recover from this illness."
—2 Kings 20:1, NLV

CHAPTER ONE

FOR THIS CAUSE:
ECCLESIAL FOUNDATIONS

Churches have a very low level of institutional self-criticism about either their purpose or the nature of their activities aimed at social reform. Like all institutions, the Black Churches have become firmly routinized in their traditions and consequently strongly resistant to internal change. A high level of devotion to their traditions and the preservation of these traditions characterize much of the life of the Churches at the denominational levels. Their capacity to encourage and to receive rigorous self-criticism in the light of their desires remains unclear.
—Peter J. Paris, The Social Teaching
of the Black Churches

I believe that God is on a mission in history to redeem creation, especially humankind. Christ's death, resurrection, and ascension constitute the heart of this mission of redemption. The Spirit is with us to lead, guide, and govern the collective witness of the Church. The Spirit informs the Church's mission to bring salvation to the world. It does this by turning non-believers into disciples. In contemporary America, this is serious work. We must pay attention to context and condition, history and identity if this work is to bear fruit.

The Greek word ekklesia connotes "Church," meaning, in general, those who are assembled or unified around the purposes and principles of God (c.f. Matt. 16:17-19; 20:25-28).[1] It is the term most often used to describe local assemblies of believers in the New Testament. It is also used in a collective sense to describe the global Church of Jesus Christ, all believers. A common alternative phrase for this second use of the word is "the body of Christ." The body of Christ is composed of all believers who will ever live (Col. 1:15-20; Eph. 1:22-23; 5:23). The local Church has a central role in shaping the personal lives of believers and equipping them for the full work of ministry. In the New Testament vision, every believer is an active part of a local Church and contributes to the collective well being of the family of God by using his or her experiences, gifts, and talents to support the vision of Christ for that work. Since Jesus came to seek and serve, persons and families called into the covenant community of Christ likewise are to be discipled to do the seeking and serving work of Jesus Christ. That is, "the Son of Man came not to be served but to serve and to give His life a ransom for many" (Mk. 10:45). Hence, each believer has a role and a responsibility to fulfill that role as a productive family member. There is no such thing as a Christian without a Church. The idea is for all ministry to be carried out under the auspices of a local Church.

EFFICIENCY VS. EFFECTIVENESS

This section could also be titled, "Doing things right vs. doing the right things." Many congregants are quite adept at doing

---

[1] According to Roy Bowen Ward, the term ekklesia occurs 114 times in the New Testament. "Ekklesia: A Word Study," Abilene Christian University, http://www.acu.edu/sponsored/restoration_quarterly/archives/1950s/vol_2_no_4_contents/ward.html. In a broad sense the ekklesia describes an "assembly." Lexicographers give as the primary meaning, "assembly duly summoned." Liddell and Scott define ekklesia as "an assembly of citizens summoned by the crier, the legislative assembly." R. Scott and H.G. Liddell, A Greek-English Lexicon (Oxford: Oxford University Press, 1935), 206. Thayer's lexicon says, "an assembly of the people convened at the public place of council for the purpose of deliberating." J. H. Thayer, A Greek-English Lexicon of the New Testament (Peabody, MA: Hendrickson, 1996), 196.

"Church work": participating in clubs, auxiliaries and ministries, sitting on boards, attending meetings, playing music, creating bulletins, and staging events. A far fewer number are actually committed to the "work of the Church": making and maturing disciples and shaping a collective witness. The journey from Church membership to discipleship can be a long, tedious process. Membership often emphasizes rights (benefits and powers derived from the organization), while discipleship places a premium on responsibility, a sacrificial ethic derived from one's relationship to Christ as the head of the Church and to His family, the Church. Church leaders who invest in the development of a missional emphasis find the emphasis on discipleship to be a more rewarding exercise. The love-ethic of Jesus Christ informs a culture of sacrifice under the supervision of doing the work of the Church, enabling individuals and families within the congregation to live out their faith with audacity, integrity, and fidelity.

In the Church in which I have served for the past ten years there has been a history of "clubs." Members gathered together around common interests and paid "dues" into their respective club treasuries. The clubs would in turn make gifts to the Church as a whole. While many members of the congregation enjoyed these "clubs" and found them meaningful, they were, in my opinion, not the best way for the Church to be a Church. The clubs encouraged the formation of cliques, and the financial needs of the larger Church were left up to the decisions of the various individual clubs. As we began to learn about tithing and investing that tithe into the work of the Church as a whole, the Church grew healthier and better able to meet both practical needs such as building maintenance as well as the needs of the community.

Budgets and buildings take up a huge slice of a congregation's creative space. It takes an incredible amount of time and effort to keep a Church building in a good state, manage the Church finances, maintain the budget, and develop Church policy. Of course these are necessary ingredients. However, the overemphasis on these items takes valuable energy, skill, and resources away from the twin tasks of disciple-making and community development. Hence, many congregations find it quite safe to shelter on the shore of tradition rather than venture out into the broad seas of social transformation and renewal. I suggest that those who shelter in place are not doing the work of the Church.

TRADITIONALISM VS. TRADITION

The past is preparation for the future. Vital congregations must mine the treasures of their collective memory in order to build a vital future. Indeed, in order to establish the conditions for a durable building enterprise, one must first build a strong foundation. Jesus is quite clear in His parable of the man who built on a rock versus the one who built on sand. Past practices of many congregations keep the memory of God's people alive; this link to a dynamic history educates and refines the present mission and identity of the Church.

Often, however, Churches are loyal to past practices that have lost their effectiveness, vitality, and relevance. For example, the aforementioned structure of "clubs" was a time-honored tradition at my Church, but had the Church members refused to let it go, it would have hurt the future of the Church. When traditions are maintained only because they are traditions, the body of Christ suffers—believers settle into a posture of unofficial boredom. Events become routinized. Stale and safe practices that appease a precious few and provide no real substance and meaning to the lives of many worshippers fuel the flaring discontent that huddles right below the surface. Clinging to traditions that are no longer relevant or meaningful, the Church as a whole maintains the status quo and inhibits the witness of the Church to the larger community.

There is a strong and important place for tradition and history in the work of the contemporary local Church, but it must be a tradition that is used as a teaching tool for present witness and future progress. The retelling of the enabling stories of spiritual rebirth and psychic rehabilitation for present-day worshipers strengthens their anticipation of God's providential presence and gracious guidance in the future.

FUNDRAISING VS. FAITH-RAISING AND FINANCIAL MANAGEMENT

Money matters. The congregation is a business. Properly run, it must adhere to sound theo-ethical principles of economics that bear witness to the covenant that we share with the rest of the creation and with God. Money matters because it is one thing to raise funds, and it is another to see long-term needs of the Church and concerns of the community met in a way that makes the Kingdom visible. Awareness of this crucial distinction is key to the success of spiritual leadership. To see money as a way to leverage the future helps congregants to plan. The work of fundraising need not be time-consuming, ill-conceived, and ill-focused. It need not drain congregants of the creative energy needed to fulfill the primary agendas of Church stewardship, discipleship, evangelism, and community building.

From the perspective of the Christian faith, economics in a general is about the conservation and amelioration of oikkonem, the cosmic order. God is passionate about creation. This world belongs to God, and God will rescue it and remake it. Oikumene and oikonome are two very closely related Greek terms that translate to ecumenism and economics. Ecumenism deals with interrelatedness, i.e. the diversity and oneness of all life. Economics has to do with how that life should be ordered, managed, and cared for. The cosmos is to be tended and cultivated. Within the house of worship, this concept is applied as stewardship, the care of the household of God—in short, economics!

Biblical principles about money pave the way for socio-economic justice. Christian stewardship, which involves the proper management and use of all of our relationships and resources, teaches that everything we do is a reflection of our relationship to the Creator. Stewardship therefore is an outworking of an inner condition. Rather than being simply about giving money to the Church, stewardship is the right response to what God has already said, done, given, and provided. It portrays for the faith community the proper organization and distribution of the tremendous array of gifts and resources that God has provided. Our righteous response begins with the recognition that God is the source and owner of all things. Our possessions should never possess us. Time, talents, treasures, and tithe are the instruments we bring to honor God in faithful response to God's gracious provision. Paul said to the Church in Philippi, "My God shall supply all your need according to his riches in glory by Christ Jesus" (Phil. 4:9). The writer of Proverbs adds, "I lead in the way of righteousness, in the midst of the paths of judgment: that I may cause those that love me to inherit substance; and I will fill their treasuries" (Prov. 8:20, 21).

What follows from this are two binding moral principles. The first is our duty to honor God with our first fruits, by which I mean prioritized giving. How we give and not just what we give is a cardinal sign of Christian maturity. According to Deuteronomic law, one purpose of tithing was to teach the people of Israel to put God first. When God is honored, our values flow from the richness of this relationship. Obedience of this kind yields innumerable rewards. A life of righteousness—of holy purpose and sanctified passion—is the insignia of such covenant faithfulness. When Churches adopt sound stewardship practices, they are in essence saying, "God's vision comes with provision." The ends and the means always cohere. Faith-raising is a matter of trust. We invest in God's program, and as shareholders in the divine economy, we are made financially healthy and responsible. The promise of divine provision and protection is realized when God is honored first in our personal and family budgets. In this way, the Church serves as a living testimony of economic justice to the world.

The second principle is that of generosity. The giving of more than what is strictly necessary or expected is a sign of trust. Just as the purchase of more stock generally typifies belief in a company's future growth and vitality, giving generously to the work of the Church implies belief in the fructifying work of the Gospel. Kingdom giving is the surest investment one can make. In the Gospel of Luke, Jesus says, "Give and it will be given to you. A good measure, pressed down, shaken together and running over, will be poured into your lap. For with the measure you use, it will be measured to you" (Luke 6:38).

Below are some Biblical practices and principles that flow from an understanding of God as the great Gift and Giver, the heart of faith-raising.

1. Teach giving practices as collective investment in God's program of salvation.

2. Select special days for the giving of offerings.

3. Teach tithing as an act of worship.

4. Connect the storehouse to the mission field; nurture community development through the giving of tithes and offerings.

5. Teach people how to handle the other 90 percent of their income.

6. Teach giving as a matter of the heart.

7. Have clear and sound financial management practices in your home and your Church.

STEWARDSHIP IN THE STOREHOUSE

For a long time, Mt. Olivet Tabernacle Baptist Church had small groups called "clubs." Each club met as its own entity, sometimes with a separate bank account. These clubs asked its members to pay dues, and this meant that each club required a treasurer. If someone wanted to give to a community project, they made a request to the treasurer who then sent the gift from the club, not necessarily from the Church as a whole.

Under the guidance of the Holy Spirit, the leaders of the Church set out to understand what the scripture teaches about God's purposes for the Church, specifically its ministries and giving. As a result, the Church shifted from a focus on clubs to a focus on ministries, from each club having its own funds to the Church having a single account to which members contributed through tithes and offerings. Club membership shifted to Church membership. Prayer, Bible study, stewardship, and giving to the Church were emphasized as a means to enrich the whole Church.

The change was initially met with some resistance. Some congregants continued to attend but intentionally and vocally withheld their tithe as a form of protest and a belief that they could control the workings of the Church. Eventually, however, this attitude faded. Now the Church has a growing endowment, financial partners, and a quarterly stewardship campaign focused exclusively on missions, evangelism, and discipleship. As one member, Sister Leach, says, "God has been faithful, and we as a Church have learned the importance of this spiritual discipline in our personal lives and in the life of the Church."

ENTERTAINMENT VS. EDIFICATION

Entertaining the congregation and filling the pews is not the primary task of the Church leadership. Rather, the proclamation of the word of God is central to the nature and mission of the Church of Jesus Christ. Not only is this critical for bringing people to Christ, but also as a tool of instruction, insight, and inspiration, the sermon provides people with the social, psychological, and professional resources to make wise choices for practical spiritual living. A good sermon encourages and directs people towards seeking out the Holy Spirit in order to make wise decisions about their tangible, daily lives. The Gospels, the Book of Acts, and the letters of Paul not only ground the New Testament's vision of the Church, but also provide a great model for the various and particular ways the Church can fulfill the ministry of the Word. Within this expansive curriculum of the New Testament, we encounter a plethora of preaching techniques: spiritual affirmation (Mt. 5); exhortation (Gal. 6; 2 Cor.13); parables (Lk. 15; Mt. 25); direct practical instruction (James 1, 2; Mt. 28:18-20); and even the use of autobiography (2 Cor. 11, 12).

Abundantly clear through these extant forms of expression is that Jesus and the early apostles steadfastly committed themselves to the conversion of individual persons and the transformation of social systems, the defeat of demonic influences and liberation from repressive cultural practices; the capacity to live free from oppressive legal codes and the responsibility to live in accordance with God's unmerited grace; the drive to be morally pure; and the sacrifice of selfish ambitions that undermine the bonds of community. Preaching in the Spirit informs the quest to live responsibly by, in, and for the Spirit. Jesus' inaugural sermon in the Gospel of Luke, rooted in Isaiah's witness, makes it plain: "The Spirit of the Lord is on me, because he has anointed me to proclaim good news to the poor" (Luke 4:18).

Many sermons intend to influence the head, while others are directed towards the heart. Sermons that relate to the head, the heart, and the hand will bring the word to life. What is a sermon if it does not move us to respond in loving-kindness to the covenant of grace established by Jesus? Purpose-driven preaching inspires, informs, and gives insight so that congregations see themselves in a new light.

PEW WARMERS VS. PRIESTHOOD OF ALL BELIEVERS

Institutional sluggishness threatens the life of many congregations. We recognize that a result of this sluggishness is our weak-willed attitude towards evangelism, discipleship, and giving. An ethic of consumerism highlights a gospel of self-fulfillment and psychic escape, hardly what Jesus required of the early disciples. In the New Testament, the Church represents the local assemblies and bodies of Christians gathered in a distinctive way in response to the grace of God as embodied in the life, work, resurrection, and ascension of Jesus Christ. Life in the Christian community is for loving persons called to relationship in Christ and given the freedom to operate in the life of the Holy Spirit (Acts 1; Mark 1:17).

We are all called be priests—to be our neighbors' keepers, healers, and friends. We are called to a ministry of healing. We are called to care for one another, to enter into relationships of mutual loving care and concern, and to develop health and restorative relationships. In Colossians 1:13-14 Paul writes, "For [Christ] delivered us from the domain of darkness, and transferred us to the kingdom of His Beloved Son, in whom we have redemption, the forgiveness of sins."

This triumphant transaction entails an inner moral transformation. In service of our heavenly King we are now endowed with new citizenship as well as new roles and responsibilities, enabling us to live beyond the limits of the ordinary.

The Gospels are replete with examples of human beings whose radical faith and unwavering hope in God empowered them to live righteously as they led others. The life of Nicodemus found new meaning after his encounter with the Christ. The woman at the well became a renowned evangelist after encountering the saving power of Jesus. The man possessed by demons was found "clothed, sitting, and in his right mind" and ran home to tell his friends (Mark 5: 15-16). Jesus gave His disciples the authority to preach, heal, and cast out demons, an endowment not attained through human means. All of these stories highlight the role of radical faith in the transformation of the believer's life, the regeneration of society, and the reformation of the Kingdom of God.

Not only does taking our role as part of the priesthood of believers move us beyond the ordinary; it also instructs us to critique unjust lifestyles and to oppose oppressive regimes. It leads us to the creation and sustenance of a more just and equitable society of fairness and respect. In short, the New Testament Church is a Church of radical discipleship and Kingdom righteousness that empowers persons in community to live as strangers in an alien world, to stand as beacons of hope, and to model nonviolence and noncooperation with evil. This type of faith takes mighty risks for God. It combats evil, brings one's life under the transforming power of the Spirit, and aligns one's actions, tone, and spirit with the peace of Christ. Jesus Christ calls us on an inward journey towards emotional wholeness as well as on an outward journey of radical righteousness. He calls us, as citizens of another Kingdom, to challenge inhumane and indecent worldly systems that create and sustain human misery.

THE CHURCH AS THE BODY OF CHRIST

The Apostle Paul presents the body as a metaphor for the diversity, unity, and equality of the Church of Jesus Christ. The body is comprised of parts, each of which relates to the whole by fulfilling its function in harmony with the others. Likewise the Church is a body of functioning members (Eph. 2:22, 23; 4:4, 15, 16). As the head of this body, Christ nurtures and nourishes that which is connected to the head: the Church. Without the headship of Christ, the body perishes. It is through this living connectedness with Christ that the Church finds the power, passion, principles, and purposes of its existence. Much like any other organism, the Church has a purpose. That purpose is to express through worship and witness the Church's fidelity to the diversity and unity of the triune God. Integration and interrelatedness are words that express both Christ and the Church that is His body. As social beings created for community, human beings are able to realize their potential if the community is healthy. The individual Christian and the congregation exist in an inescapable body of mutual obligation. All who have received the Spirit are to partake in this dynamic unity.

CHAPTER TWO

I SHALL GIVE YOU SHEPHERDS:

PASTORAL CARE AND PRAYER

For God did not appoint us to suffer wrath but to receive salvation through our Lord Jesus Christ. He died for us so that, whether we are awake or asleep, we may live together with him. Therefore encourage one another and build each other up, just as in fact you are doing.
—*1 Thess. 5:9–11*

Be shepherds of God's flock that is under your care, watching over them—not because you must, but because you are willing, as God wants you to be; not pursuing dishonest gain, but eager to serve; not lording it over those entrusted to you, but being examples to the flock. And when the Chief Shepherd appears, you will receive the crown of glory that will never fade away.
—*1 Pet. 5:2–4*

A new command I give you: Love one another. As I have loved you, so you must love one another. By this everyone will know that you are my disciples, if you love one another.
—*John 13:34-35*

The aim of this chapter is to explore Jesus as the model of compassionate servant leadership. I believe that the central task of the servant leaders is to give the gift of ourselves in service to the witness of Christ, the Lord of the universe. The pastor serves as gift giver in three essential roles: serving, caring, and praying.

THE GIFT OF SERVING

The thirteenth chapter of John introduces the upper room discourse in which, after partaking of the Passover, Jesus performs the menial task of washing the feet of the disciples, illustrating the central Gospel teaching of servant leadership. This event is not included in any other Gospel account. John 13:1 provides the context to us from the beginning: "Jesus knew that the hour had come." This is the eve of the crucifixion. Jesus was going to the cross as a sacrifice for humanity. He was innocent, the threat of hell loomed, but Jesus displayed great spiritual and mental focus as He concentrated on serving, loving, and gathering His followers to himself. Even with death around the corner, Christ did not waver. He did not panic or lose faith. He displayed His love ethic in the form of foot washing. The sacrifice expressed by this act with towel and basin embodied His life and teachings and foreshadowed His ultimate act of sacrificial love displayed at Calvary. Matthew 20:28 says He came "not to be served, but to serve, and to give His life as a ransom for many."

Several things emerge from this text. First, Jesus became a servant in order to show love to His disciples and by extension the rest of humanity. Secondly, Jesus' sacrificial act supplies the supreme model of Kingdom righteousness. The lowly work of foot washing is both transformative and progressive. It is transformative because it denies the posture that keeps me alienated from my neighbor. It repudiates fear and forges a connection. Through cleansing, true trust is cultivated—an attitude that indicates the breakdown of false barriers. It is progressive because it opens up pathways to vital new relationships. Thirdly, the images of the towel and the basin model to the world that the power of love is superior to the love of power. Love keeps the needs of one's neighbor foremost in one's life. It demonstrates the power of authentic relationships. With a "coalition of evil" forming against Him, Jesus never wavers from His original commitment to serve the Father and build authentic human community.

The task of servanthood is more often than not unglamorous and unpopular. Most people do not aspire to be something associated with lowliness, sacrifice, longsuffering, self-effacement, and, yes, hard work. Little wonder than in an age of entitlement most people aspire to be celebrities, scholars, experts and visionaries but not servants. Jesus is the chief exemplar of such an ethic.

The kind of servanthood embodied by Jesus is unpopular precisely because it is unselfish. This model of servanthood exemplifies the deepest kind of compassion, the selfless sacrificial renunciation of the will for the sake of another's benefit. Christ's act becomes the scarlet thread of the Gospel, the self-abnegation that is the chosen path of righteousness of the one who made Himself of no reputation. Of course this is no easy task. Bonhoeffer once wrote, "When Christ calls a man, He bids him come and die."[1] Likewise Dr. King said, "The ultimate test of a man is not where he stands in moments of comfort and moments of convenience, but where he stands in moments of challenge and moments of controversy."[2] The garment of servanthood is woven with hardship, turbulence, uncertainty, and conflict. In this sense servanthood and discipleship are inseparable. In order to be a disciple one must carry one's

---

1 Dietrich Bonhoeffer, The Cost of Discipleship (New York: Touchstone, 1959), 89.
2 Martin Luther King, Jr., Untitled Speech at Nobel Peace Prize Recognition Dinner, (Speech, Atlanta, GA, January 27, 1965), The King Center. http://www.thekingcenter.org/archive/document/mlk-speech-nobel-peace-prize-recognition-dinner.

cross, bear unbearable burdens, and be willing to go where one has never been and do what one has never done.

Here is where many potentially great relationships never get off the ground, and this is also true for pastors and their congregations. So many disciples of Christ never fully develop because they buy the lie that good relationships happen only when we find the person or people who will meet our needs as we would like them to. We mistakenly think we will have a great marriage if we find the right spouse who will cater to our every desire. We will have best friends if we find the people who always meet our emotional needs. We will have great family relationships if our family will just understand our wants and desires. We will have a great Church when our congregation is energetic and creative. We wait for this perfect utopia where all our needs are going to be met by the people around us. When all the planets and stars line up, and all the right people are meeting our needs, then suddenly we will find "relationship paradise." Or so we think. But the Garden of Eden has long passed due to man's sinful nature, so many of us sit forlornly, wondering why we have no close relationships here on earth.

Jesus' ethic of service undermines traditional ways of operating, and it is oppositional to a worldly ethic that seeks status over sacrifice and greed over giving. Yet the practice of foot washing highlights another aspect of ministry—the ethic of care giving that builds authentic relationships and keeps us connected to others in creative and compassionate ways. A congregation that understands this care giving as modeled by their pastors and leaders will more effectively live out an ethic of servanthood in the communities in which they live, offering a picture of Jesus to their neighbors that reflects both salvation and social change.

THE GIFT OF CARING

The moral crisis that threatens our collective well-being is thick, amoebic, and multilayered. Not only does it show up on large-scale social catalogs of crime, homelessness, ineffective public schools, economic decline, and political corruption, but it has personal and family indices as well. It is quite unsettling to listen to and observe the tragic and heroic personal stories of individuals who are caged by these hostile forces. These accounts deepen and dramatize the more framed accounts of the urban analysts, activists, and policymakers who have lamented the decline of the three-legged stool upon which so much of urban America rests: Church, family, and school. Nibbling away at the core of these issues is an erosion of substantive moral and authentic psychological relationships, as well as a fraying of long-standing supportive networks that heretofore upheld persons and families and the congregations in community with them.

Within the urban crucible of broken families, learning deprivation, severe individual alienation, trauma, and domestic abuse, the need for a well-honed ethic of pastoral care can hardly be overestimated. The spiritual leader is often called upon to reshape the moral atmosphere of the community. More often than not this requires the investment of a large amount of time in addressing the pressing personal needs of others. For persons who are negotiating a broad sweep of personal crises such as divorce, harassment, physical and mental illness, and unemployment, it is important that pastors actually offer care. This may include teaching the Great Commandment to individuals and families as well as teaching believers to love others as they love themselves and to show their love for God in their love of others. When love is not felt, or when supportive networks disappear, feelings of alienation, personal failure, and animosity towards community result. In a culture where status and self-identity mean so much, not to have a sense of belonging is a profound social disability.

Our desire for status and expression is addictive, and we will look at some of the implications of this in our urban communities in Part Two. Yet it is also elusive. When the quest for status is shattered, when our false sense of stability and invincibility crumbles, alienation sets in, a state in which we feel naked, alone, and unprotected against life's assaults. Despair is the natural consequence. It is difficult to live with brokenness. The human psyche shudders at the prospect of not achieving its desires. No matter how much our culture of "me" is trumpeted and championed, ultimately there is no haven to escape the pitfalls of life—illness, divorce, being laid off, losing a loved one, foreclosing on a home.

Under such conditions people cry out for a ministry of care and concern. It is not that the pastor can provide the answers, for there are few easy answers to life's problems. The pastor simply points the way to a "well that never runs dry." All may drink of its life-giving waters. Only a pastor immersed in the tragic though triumphant worlds of others and who is connected to their trials and brokenness can serve as a conduit of grace that flows from this well. This, my friends, is hardly Herculean work, but it is holy work. Only the holy force of God's Spirit can aid pastor and people in such a work of compassion. Addressing the wounds of those left for dead on the Jericho road is the starting point of transformation.

Spiritual leaders must constantly work to forge relationships based on care. The work of relationship building is tedious. It is riddled with risk and restlessness, anxiety and awkwardness. But it carries with it enormous potential for transformation and, ultimately, reward. It requires the fruit of the Spirit—patience, forgiveness, grace, and self-examination. Spiritual leaders who seek to bring their people to the place where God desires them to be must learn to do so in the trenches. A caring touch in feeding and leading requires a degree of vulnerability that not many are willing to experience.

Spiritual leaders are caregivers. They are called to be shepherds, not CEOs, board directors, celebrities, military generals, or absentee landlords. The work of a shepherd requires a special kind of caregiving that demands patience, sacrifice, and soulful attention. The task of shepherding requires stability, reliability, and integrity. It involves time, energy, attention, and, above all, love. Caregiving is the substance of fellowship. The more one loves and prays for the congregation as a whole, the more one grows in love for them, and the more one grows in creativity and resourcefulness in attending to their manifold needs. However, the weight of the vision is too heavy, burdensome, and complicated for one person to carry alone; pastors must learn to balance the weight. The congregation has an obligation to grow in grace as caregivers as well.

I thank my God every time I remember you. In all my prayers for all of you, I always pray with joy because of your partnership in the Gospel from the first day until now, being confident of this, that he who began a good work in you will carry it on to completion until the day of Christ Jesus. (Phil 1:3-6)

The shepherd, as caregiver, models God's love for humanity to the congregation, and the congregation in turn models this love to the lost and the left. Guided by the Spirit, the prayers of pastor and people spread abroad the love of God. God's love for us is communicated in the power of the Holy Spirit. Likewise our love for God is mediated by Christ and communicated in the power of the Holy Spirit. The result is a mutual love among human beings, again mediated by Christ in the power of the Holy Spirit.

THE GIFT OF PRAYING

The pastor is a chief conduit of God's grace. As the pastor and other spiritual leaders sincerely seek God's will, the spirit of godliness envelops the Church community. The Church is then sent out to a dying world through worship, work, witness, and the winning of souls. Prayer is the way that we enter ever more deeply into the fellowship of the Trinity. Prayer is not an individualistic matter but the work of the whole Christian community. In order to be pastoral caregivers we must allow the biblical image and Spirit of God as scripture to govern our commitments. The living faith that we reflect allows us to be conduits of grace in other persons, families, or groups in their moments of vulnerability or concern. As we pray we help others negotiate life's problems by teaching them: "Cast all your anxieties on [God], for he cares about you" (1 Pet. 5:7).

The Church is the school of prayer for the entire world. Jesus said, "My house will be called a house of prayer for all nations" (Mark 11:17).[3] Its vitality is expressed in its power to create the inner revolution of the heart—propelling its movement towards God. As the old folk are fond of saying, "Prayer may not always change your situation, but it will change you in your situation." The change of perspective, attitude, and belief wrought by our prayers brings us deeper into the life of God, the redeemer of the universe. Prayer is the currency of eternity. It echoes deep in the inner recesses of the heart. Seen in this manner, we the Church are called and created to intercede for the universe (Mt. 24:14; Ps. 111:6; Phil. 2:10; Isa. 61:11; Hab. 2:14). What an incredible honor!

The Bible teaches us that what we utter to God echoes our perspectives, practices, and behaviors. The pastor as chief intercessor is called to hear and speak the language of the Spirit—to intercede for others on the basis of their needs and concerns,

---

3 See also: John 2:14-17; Mt. 21:12-13; Mark 11:15-17; Luke 19:45-46; Mal. 3:1-3.

hurts, and foibles. Through prayer the pastor leads the Church to give witness to the loving God of grace who sustains and renews our lives. Prayer engages the Church in a sacred practice because at its best it is the very definition of being a person of God. Without prayer the relationship is at risk, and thus one's very identity as a believer.

Prayer is a relational act. It is an activity of the whole being—spirit, mind, and soul. This is because prayer is the act by which the carnal demands of the flesh surrender to God. Prayer is letting God set the agenda for our lives and our ministries. As prayer focuses the human heart on the divine will, we experience creativity: light is brought out of darkness. The result is the radical transformation of our attitudes, behaviors, and relationships. We come to resemble the one whose will became flesh in order to transform persons, congregations, and institutions. Prayer in this sense translates the wisdom of God in ways that turn the world upside down. For "God chose the foolish things of the world to shame the wise; God chose the weak things of the world to shame the strong" (1 Cor. 1:27). Prayer creates a synergy between God and the congregants, permitting access to the power and grace of heaven in order to transform the earth. Prayer therefore is not so much about getting folks into heaven; it is about getting the power of heaven down to earth.[4]

Through prayer congregations become drawn to God's purposes. They combine the work of the Great Commission and the work of the Great Commandment. Prayer is the key weapon against human hopelessness, helplessness, and haplessness, the triumvirate evils that destroy human personality and community. Prayer brings life to the dead and hope to the despondent. It is water, bread, and life.

---
[4] Ps. 39:12; 71:2; 119:170; 140:6; Mt. 26:36-46; 27:46; Luke 3:21-22; 9:28-29; 23:34,46.

Through prayer, lives are changed for the better, communities are healed, crime is reduced, school systems are delivered, families are saved, businesses are established, cities become better dwelling places, and entire nations redirect their ways (2 Chr. 7:14). Without prayer, the mighty machinery of the universe is life-crushing. Prayer is how we participate in the work of God. The prayer of the faithful shall heal the world. We are invited to enter into the vineyard of prayer so that we may abide with the true vine and be cared for by the vinedresser. We know that no other force in the universe can move those things that are not aligned with their purpose to glorify God like prayer can. Prayer, then, is our oxygen. It allows us to breathe in the very breath (ruah) of God in ways that give meaning and inspiration to people's lives. In John 14:13–14 Jesus said, "And I will do whatever you ask in my name, so that the Father may be glorified in the Son. You may ask me for anything in my name, and I will do it."

Prayer begins with the character of God. As we direct our attention to the heart and character of God, we become inspired, and yes, even intoxicated by God's power to move. One way to focus our attention on God is to read and to become familiar with God's great exploits: How God made the heavens and the earth. How God called Abraham. How God gave Sarah a child. How God parted the Red Sea. How God through Jesus fed the five thousand with five loaves and two fish. How God through Jesus raised Lazarus from the dead. By rehearsing the enabling stories and seminal events of the Bible, our faith grows. It strengthens a healthy Church and immunizes us against the sin of unbelief and disobedience. So we pray the prayer of faith, knowing that God can move mountains.

Of course the alternative to making God the center and circumference of our prayer efforts is to allow our attention and energies to be absorbed by the human predicament. When this is our first move, we relegate God to the margins of our perspective.

We make God small. We are not afforded the full riches of divine fellowship, and we are deprived of the strength, vitality, and peace that make life meaningful and productive. It is part of our Christian duty to be aware of the predicaments in our communities, especially when so many are common to urban America, but our prayers about these predicaments should always include the truth of the scripture that tells us of the goodness and greatness of God. When prayer begins with a focus on our problems and predicaments, then we are limited to what we can do and endure in our woefully limited lives. Prayers made in this way are bricks without straw, lanterns without oil, salt that has lost its taste. They are mere words, empty utterances of feeling that fill the empty spaces. The greatness of God and His power is the sum and source of prayer.
E. M. Bounds reminds us that:

> *Prayer puts God's work in His hands, and keeps it there. It looks to Him constantly and depends on Him implicitly to further His own cause. Prayer is but faith resting in, acting with, and leaning on and obeying God. This is why God loves it so well, why He puts all power into its hands, and why He so highly esteems people of prayer.*[5]

Prayer opens up the human mind to the infinite possibilities and manifold blessings of the Kingdom. As prayer connects us to God, we become Christ-like. Through this process we understand what God wants us to learn and how to advance this work of redemption on earth.

Pastors pray for their people. Prayer is the one essential element that aids spiritual leaders in their efforts to forge congregational health and growth. As the pastor's heart opens up to the resources and riches of divine fellowship, the flock of God becomes nearer and dearer. Through being educated in the ways of the Spirit,

---
[5] E.M. Bounds, E.M. Bounds on Prayer, Harold Chadwick, ed. (Orlando: Bridge-Logos Publishers, 2001), 401.

the work of the Spirit becomes less of a burden or at least a joint burden to bear. The pastor can move into a place where he/she is better able to meet the congregants at their place of need. Prayer helps pastors to develop the heart of God that highlights their shepherding function: to lead God's people into a loving relationship with Him. Prayer is the primary vehicle to this end (1 Pet. 5:2; John 21:16; Acts 20:28-29).

In the sixth chapter of Acts we read of a spectacular moment in which the Church leaders engage in a division of labor: the ministers are freed up for prayer and ministry of the Word. Without the energy of prayer, pastors are powerless to affect change in the world and to inspire their congregations. Without the enlightenment of the pastor, the flock may go astray and become a hindrance to the Gospel. Without speaking faith and hearing from God, the spiritual leadership becomes a rudderless ship, tossed to and fro by every new fad and whim. Prayer anchors us to the heart of God.

Prayer draws us close to God by bringing us into alignment with His will. Prayer energizes us with the power of belief, allowing us to walk by faith and not by sight. Prayer makes us rest with God because it monitors our faith, whose primary function is to please God. God is able to bless us above anything we can ask or think. Only powerful focus on who we are and whom we serve will cure our feeblemindedness. Our societies are flooded by crises; mayhem seems to be the order of things. Crime, domestic abuse, family dysfunction, rampant divorce, brokenness, mounting violence, bureaucratic inertia, myopic religion and even demonic attacks wage a frontal assault on the Kingdom of God. Our congregation and communities are "waiting to exhale." We need God to heal our Churches, communities, cities, and conventions. Spiritual leaders are depressed and more often than not leading dysfunctional systems. We need more than formal educations, well-heeled programming, expert fundraising techniques, and formal discipleship programs.

We need God to breathe on us; we need to experience our first love. We need a miracle in order for us to do the thing were called to do in this age. We must be bold enough to approach the throne of God so that the miracle that takes place in us creates the world, and specifically our urban communities, anew.

The spiritual fellowship to which we are called invites us into intimate communion with God and with one another. Life in the Church is meant to mirror the mutual indwelling of and fellowship with the Holy Trinity. Serving, caring, and prayer are essential to this purpose and critical for health in the community. Miraculous experiences develop through the gifts of prayer, serving, and caring, for it is through this sacred vehicle that we enjoy the fullest communion with the Spirit of God. This fellowship allows us to serve and care for our congregations and communities while we endure life's struggles and hardships.

CHAPTER THREE

YE SHALL RECEIVE POWER:

THE HOLY SPIRIT AND THE CHURCH AS COMMUNITY OF COMPASSION

> *The Holy Spirit also personally enables Messiah's followers to proclaim His Gospel to the nations. Like the prophets of old, their decentralized universal worship of God under the New Covenant is mediated by the Holy Spirit under Messiah's authority.*
> —Walt Russell [1]

> *God whispers to us in our pleasures, speaks in our conscience, but shouts in our pains: it is His megaphone to rouse a deaf world.*
> —C. S. Lewis, The Problem of Pain

The Messiah's long-awaited arrival brings with it the promise of the coming New Age, one that is marked by peace, justice, and moral flourishing for all Israel. Yet Jesus' "baptism of the Spirit" also signals the inauguration of the much-anticipated Messianic age that begins with Israel and is shared with all nations of the earth, signaling the inclusivity of God's covenant with all

---

[1] Walt Russell, "The Holy Spirit's Ministry in the Fourth Gospel." Grace Theological Journal 8, no. 2 (September 1, 1987): 227-239.

humanity.[2] Subscribers to this New Age, "those born from above" (John 3), are partakers of divine grace (John 17), and through belief are dynamically and continuously empowered by the Spirit to bring salvation to a world that hangs in the balance. The outpouring of the Spirit is the promised precursor of the Messianic movement, supplying spiritual license to the Holy Nation. Holding the blood-stained banner of love and peace, the Church is the New Israel sent to call gentile peoples to repentance.

FROM INCARNATION TO PENTECOST

The key event in all of history, next to the incarnation, death, and resurrection of Jesus Christ, is the giving of the Comforter by the Messiah. At the incarnation, God became flesh in a way that shares radical light and love with human beings. He dwelt among us "full of grace and truth" (John 1:14). In the incarnation we find the blueprint for how God, in Christ, saves human beings—the graphic picture of salvation. Dietrich Bonhoeffer writes:

> *It is the image of one who enters a world of sin and death, who takes upon Himself all the sorrows of humanity, who meekly bears God's wrath and judgment against sinners, and obeys His will with unswerving devotion in suffering and death, the man born to poverty, the friend of publicans and sinners, the man of sorrows, rejected of man, and forsaken of God. Here is God made man, here is the man in the new image of God.* [3]

At Pentecost, the promised inauguration of the nascent Christian community is cast both publicly and in the presence of a representative host of global witnesses. The Holy Spirit carries on the work of Christ through those He calls and sends for this singular purpose. The irenic purpose of the Church is known only

---

2 Is. 11:1-2; 42:148; Ez. 18:31; 36:25-27; 37:14; 39:39; Joel 2:28-32.
3 Michael Van Dyke, Radical Integrity: The Story of Dietrich Bonhoeffer (Uhrichsville, OH: Barbour Press, 2001), 115.

through the Spirit's illumination of the Scriptures. The apostle Paul wonderfully defines the assembly of believers as "called according to His purpose" (Romans 8:28). The mission of the Church flows from the mission and message of Jesus. The Church, therefore, is not a human organization, even though it is entrusted to human hands. It is an organization specifically created, sustained, and nurtured by God to fulfill God's purposes on earth. And it is only through the Spirit that the Church has life.

The Spirit informs and inspires the global mission of the ekklesia, ushering in the fulfillment of the Great Commission and protecting it from the deadly poisons of a fallen and wicked world. The world cannot understand the Spirit, because in its fallenness and fleshiness it rails against the reign of God. The grammar and logic of the Spirit can only be understood through the radical event of the cross, an act of selflessness, unmerited love, and unrivaled courage. The world, overridden with pride and pretension, conflict and competition, alienation and aggression, builds monuments to what is perishing rather than to what is ultimate. Human beings under its sway look for meaning in broken cisterns and thus are devoid of the Living Water that quenches all thirst.

The Spirit, then, is both custodian and guardian of the Holy Nation. Without the Spirit's guardianship our witness is "seed among thorns," a lukewarm social organization, an unvarnished assemblage of human beings, a misguided moral compass. The Church ushers the world into its promised hope. Absent of the Holy Spirit, the body of Christ is vulnerable to its own pretensions and exposed to the nefarious darts of a world set against the Kingdom. To put it crudely, it is a fallen corpse, a body without breath. Invariably, the Spirit separates the City of God from the fallen cities of this world. Through the Spirit's witness the Church remains that institutional reality that abides with Christ, who is unassailably at its head. The Church therefore provides the world a brilliant social model based on its distinctive story in Christ, which is the New Testament. When the Church swerves from its central purpose, when it evades its mission, it is the Spirit who serves as an agent of conversion, calling it back to the foundational terms of its covenant as the body of Christ. This act of integration is a key function of the Spirit in the life of the individual Christian and the Christian community.

The sending of the Holy Spirit begins with a particular community and through its progressive witness spreads to every culture and nation. The Church is called to minister the Gospel of Christ to the entirety of creation. Only the Spirit can supervise the complex and colossal enterprise of sanctifying the work of the Great Commission, folding the specific errand for Israel into the Gospel of Christ for all nations. In this providential sweep of the Spirit, the Church is to be an assembly of holiness and righteousness for all peoples—a light to the gentiles. All are invited and welcomed into the banquet of grace, to be part of the family of the faith. The unifying work of the Spirit among different cultures does not homogenize, squash, or flatten cultural specificity. Rather, it speaks to varying needs and patterns of the different communities, allowing all to sing the chorus of God within their various tongues and tones.

The Holy Spirit works both within and beyond human comprehension. In one way, the Spirit accommodates human agency by making its grammar conformable to reason. Simultaneously, the Spirit's ways are incomprehensible and sometimes unidentifiable, its fruits only made manifest within the "fullness of time," creatively concretized within the life of the individual believer and within a particular congregation's witness to its generation and culture (Acts 1:8). It is the Spirit that enables the Church to do evangelism, make disciples (Acts 1:5), perform healing acts, provide ministries of mercy, become a witness of peace in the world, fight for justice, take care of the homeless and the orphans, and shape the public ethos of civil society. Through the redemptive and regenerative work of the Spirit, Christians become authentic witnesses to the promises, powers, and presence of Christ. The Spirit protects the Church from the world even as it overcomes the world through unity, faith, and love. "And you shall be my witnesses in Judaea, Samaria and to the ends of the earth" (Acts 1:8). This means that God is always the first and last word, encouraging both believer and believing community to do the impossible.

AND YE SHALL RECEIVE POWER: THE SUBSTANCE OF OUR WITNESS

Life is never the same again for the person who becomes part of the covenant community of the faithful. The Holy Spirit "seals" the believer in Christ, safeguarding salvation. This new life lease, signed by a pen dipped in grace, involves release from the burden of meaningless suffering into the rewards of creative suffering, given to those who are resolved to live out the faith. Flowing from posture of life-giving courage is a profound appreciation for the relationship with one who is both Gift and Giver. But there is more. And this point cannot be overemphasized: This new experience invites an inversion of one's values, a call to spiritual arms against the self, and a moral conversion. This is what the framers of the New Testament pointedly referred to with the Greek word metanoia. It is the definitive call of grace, the invitation to the radical life of faith, a dramatic change that inaugurates the "cost of discipleship." These words of an old song aptly dramatize the moral forcefulness of the crippled that become Christ-like: "The things I used to do, I don't do anymore. The places I used to go, I don't go anymore." The point is this: I shall "go and sin no more" (John 8:11).

Despite fallen human perceptions and inclinations—impulses that give birth to the sins of pride and sensuality—God willfully calls the "defective and dejected" to manifest His will on earth. Jesus deploys the most unlikely and unseemly to bring the impossible into fruition. The sovereign will of the Triune God of grace knows no bounds. Jehovah's rhetorical probing of Moses accents the infinite scope of this inscrutable providential searching: "Who gave human beings their mouths? Who makes them deaf or mute? Who give them sight or makes them blind? Is it not I, the Lord?" (Ex. 4:11).

The Holy Spirit not only rescues sinners from damnation, desperation, and death, but invests in them the sacred responsibility of life: moral duty. The Kingdom of Heaven requires its citizens to participate in the passion of Christ, but this citizenship cannot be coerced. It is offered freely, not grudgingly, an invitation to be rejected or received: "Here I am! I stand at the door and knock" (Rev. 3:20). And the one who answers takes on the responsibility of being Christ's co-laborer. The God of the covenant community cannot act otherwise. Surrender is an indication of the conviction to accept the "price" for change and the desire to join this creative relationship. As transformed beings, we participate in the transformation of present reality as forerunners of hope: we become the ekklesia—agents of the Spirit of God. In a word: missionaries.

THE HOLY SPIRIT AND THE UNIVERSAL SPREAD OF THE GOSPEL MISSION

The Holy Spirit reveals God to the Church and to the world (John 14:26). The splendid task of unveiling the character and will of Jesus is the sole responsibility of the Spirit. Simultaneously, the Spirit participates progressively in the life of the community it reveals, forging the biography of the Church, an enterprise that involves the selective unveiling of different aspects of God's nature in overcoming the challenges of the Church in fulfilling its mission. The Spirit desires that the life shaped by gratitude becomes the central ingredient in the life of the Church. The Holy Spirit allows us to know and participate in the life of Jesus, leading us to become partakers in the divine image. In this sense, the Holy Spirit performs the work of conversion and sanctification in the life of the believer and the Church.

The Church is the Lord's instrument of peace, the vehicle in history of the Missio Dei. Its central emphasis on evangelism as the midwife of salvation is complemented by the work of discipleship. Hence, evangelism (bringing people into the faith) and ethics (bringing people up in the faith) are two sides of the same salvific coin. Congregations are required not only to bring people to Christ but also to help them to mature in faith. Discipleship is a special task with its own curriculum. The goal of discipleship is the development of a mature believer in Christ: one who is Christ-like in belief and behavior and who stands as a city upon a hill. The Spirit directs the work of the Church, and the Church partakes in the work of the Spirit.

Paul says to the Church in Philippi:

> *And this is my prayer: that your love may abound more and more in knowledge and depth of insight, so that you may be able to discern what is best and may be pure and blameless for the day of Christ, filled with the fruit of righteousness that comes through Jesus Christ—to the glory and praise of God. (Phil. 1:9-11)*

And in Colossians 3:1-3, he writes:

> *Since, then, you have been raised with Christ, set your hearts on things above, where Christ is, seated at the right hand of God. Set your minds on things above, not on earthly things. For you died, and your life is now hidden with Christ in God.*

The Church, then, is the agent of salvation in its proclamation and its practice. The Spirit inspires faith (Rom. 8:15; Gal. 4:6). "Without faith it is impossible to please God" (Heb. 11:6). Faith is living in such a way that God's purposes become my purposes. In this way I am conformed to God's will. Faith is also living courageously in the face of opposition. It is the capacity to follow God even when we cannot see where He is leading.

As a re-presentative of Christ to a dying world, the Spirit functions as the "instrument of peace." The living reality of such magnificent witness is that in a real sense practice is a form of proclamation, and proclamation is a form of practice. Moreover, the Church shines forth the light of Christ both in terms of how it represents itself externally to the world and how it honors Christ through its internal workings, operations, and structure (John 16:14). Individual persons, grounded in the life of the Spirit within the Church, bear the fruit of their relationship with Christ (Gal. 5:22-23). They are made into witnesses of Christ through the Spirit's liberating influence (Rom. 8:2). In short, their discipleship is productive. They bear the fruit of the Spirit. These fruit, given only by the Holy Spirit, are undeniable marks of the Spirit's express workings, underscoring the work of sanctification that guides the Church as it grows towards health, wholeness, and maturity.

The Spirit then educates disciples of the truth about their relationship in Christ (John 16:13). The Spirit's empowering truth and presence enables disciples to perform impossible acts in the face of teeming opposition. The Spirit fights and overcomes sin and calls us into holy living: "When He comes, He will prove the world to be in the wrong about sin and righteousness and judgment" (John 16:8). This conviction leads to our calling to hearing, holiness, and helping (1 Pet. 1:23). The New Testament underscores the believer's new citizenship in a Kingdom not of this world; one whose author and founder is God. Peter reminds his audience they are "a chosen people, a royal priesthood, a holy nation, God's special possession, that [they] may declare the praises of Him who called [them] out of darkness into wonderful light" (1 Pet. 2:9; see also Rom. 9:24). Hence, the Spirit is Christ's presence in every believer.

Every Church that convicts the world of sin instills in the Christian a deep sense of calling, comforts the brokenhearted, and challenges the believing community to perform the supernatural acts of compassion, mercy, and justice. "For the Spirit God gave us does not make us timid, but gives us power, love, and self-discipline" (2 Tim. 1:7).

LIVING IN THE SPIRIT: BEARING FRUIT

The fact that the Spirit brings human beings into the economy of salvation implies a supreme order, an unvarnished logic. The logic of the Spirit communes with the will of God, which constitutes the design and destiny of the cosmos. That this logic is not fully grasped by the human mind dramatizes rather than denies its authority. Its autonomy inheres in its mystery. The inscrutability of the Spirit is only inscrutable from the human point of view. From the divine vantage point it is definite, composite, and yet unbridled and unassailable. God delivers; we discern. In this way, God "accommodates" us. The mysterious logic of the Spirit can only be rightly apprehended through faith. This is part of the terrible and terrific life of the Spirit—the *mysterium tremendum*![4] It both grounds our faith and anticipates the future hope that is Christ's coming. The logic is not simply a pattern; it is the word spoken, the impulse, the energy, the drama of the Spirit. According to Martin Bucer:

> *So those who believe are not under the law, because they have the Spirit within them, teaching them everything more perfectly*

---

4 Rudolph Otto developed this idea in his magisterial work The Idea of the Holy. He is worth quoting at length: We are dealing with something for which there is only one appropriate expression, mysterium tremendum. . . . The feeling of it may at times come sweeping like a gentle tide pervading the mind with a tranquil mood of deepest worship. It may pass over into a more set and lasting attitude of the soul, continuing, as it were, thrillingly vibrant and resonant, until at last it dies away, and the soul resumes its "profane," non-religious mood of everyday experience. . . It has its crude, barbaric antecedents and early manifestations, and again it may be developed into something beautiful and pure and glorious. It may become the hushed, trembling, and speechless humility of the creature in the presence of—whom or what? In the presence of that which is a Mystery inexpressible and above all creatures." The Idea of the Holy, tr. J.W. Harvey (New York: OUP, 1923); full text online.

than the law ever could and motivating them much more powerfully to obey it. In other words, the Holy Spirit moves the heart, so the believers wish to live by those things which the law commands, but which the law could not achieve by itself. [5]

Freedom, then, is an unquestionable mark of the Spirit. It is a substantive liberty that raises spiritual maturity over personal desire. As such it is not simply freedom from, but a freedom to and a freedom for. It is a confidence birthed by our citizenship in God's new buoyant polity.

Freedom gives birth to the fruit of the Spirit, which may be seen as "rights" of living in the Kingdom of righteousness. Just as upstanding citizens in a constitutional democracy have the inalienable "right" to life, no one can deny the believer the "right" to love or the "right" to hope. In short, one has the "right" to live for Christ. Paul put it summarily, "For me to live is Christ and to die is gain" (Phil. 1:21).[6]

Life with the Spirit is a dangerous and wrenching affair. Spiritual living is risky living. It demands that I starve the egotism that attends my glib self-assurance and my blind narcissism. Often in our Churches we continue traditions or patterns long after their period of effectiveness or usefulness simply because that is the way it has always been done. A Church in tune with the Holy Spirit

---

[5] Alister McGrath, Christian Theology: an Introduction (West Sussex, UK: John Wiley and Sons, 2011), 232.

[6] The fruit of the spirit as "rights" both defend and deepen the believer's citizenship in the bourgeoning reign of God. To be sure, the fruit is not a "birth right" merited by our own ingenuity or initiative. It is the unmerited and priceless gift of grace, the result of the Spirit's labor. Spiritual fruit serves as a double witness: as the mark of the Holy Spirit as source and as the result of a life surrendered to Jesus. Borne out of the life of obedience, the fruit of the Spirit squash the demands of the ego, a feat unachievable by human power. My noblest actions carry with them an egoistic impulse, for I hide my pretense in the shadow of self-congratulation. The surrendered life pays the costs of discipleship and says, "Let not my will but thy will be done." Strength is wrought in weakness, keeping the cross the ultimate prize in all aspects of life. To deny this cardinal truth is to risk penalty and peril. The Spirit, then, brokers the friendship between me and the cross.

will be sensitive to the Spirit's leading in regards to changing structures, programs, and other traditions within that particular congregation.

As the Spirit introduces me to myself, I emerge from hiding, I heal, and I am reborn. Tendencies to deceive and manipulate are purged or at least kept in check. Surrender to the life of the Spirit involves a retraction, a re-education of my world-soaked, intractably carnal value system. The Spirit seeks to divest me of years of negative indoctrination about personal self-fulfillment, upward mobility, and financial opportunity in a modern capitalist society. Idolatrous lifestyles, the hunt for endless stimulation, and the boundlessness of our egoistic hedonism subtly conspire to produce a parasitic culture of carnivorous individualism. Spiritual homicide and suicide can only be halted by the creative work of the Spirit that revises my need to "make it." When I put my needs, goals, and aspirations at the top of the agenda, I partake unwittingly in the crucifixion of our Lord. I grieve the Spirit and am led away from spiritual wellness, forging a descent into destruction, for it means that I deny myself both my source and my destiny.

It is in response to the call of the Church that the believer finds the stamina to live fearlessly for the Kingdom. Owing singularly to this passion of belonging to Christ, the disciple realizes the effective power of God to create a new people, a revitalized community capable of bearing the cross amidst human wretchedness and wickedness. The Spirit transforms us into the community of Christ by making us a risk-taking community, the radical people of the cross. This is the unadulterated meaning of being with Christ—a task impossible without the Spirit. Through the patent of Christ's love we are brought into the covenant, embracing and embodying a way of life that God has made possible here and now. The Holy Spirit seals our citizenship in the new eschatological community of "amazing grace." The Church received power through the Spirit's compassion, and in its free offering of this compassion to others receives more power. It is only in the giving of compassionate energy formed in grace and birthed by the Spirit that the Church becomes stronger and holier. A loving community dedicated to peace, righteousness, and justice is the mark of the Spirit's call upon our lives.

CHAPTER FOUR

MAKING IT PLAIN:
THE VISION IMPERATIVE

Vision is the art of seeing the invisible.
—Jonathan Swift

Vision leads to venture, and history is on the side of venturesome faith. The person of vision takes fresh steps of faith across gullies and chasms, not "playing safe" but neither taking foolish risks.
—J. Oswald Sanders, Spiritual Leadership

It is very dangerous to go into eternity with possibilities which one has oneself prevented from becoming realities. A possibility is a hint from God. One must follow it.
—Soren Kierkegaard, The Soul of Kierkegaard

Create your future from your future, not your past.
—Werner Erhard

Where there is no vision the people perish.
Prov. 29:18

Vision is holy and human, eternal and temporal, immediate and gradual, personal and public. It is a venture into the vast resources of God's plan. Once a people catch the fire, so to speak, they begin to trust where God is leading, a spirit of expectancy sets in, and all happenings—even flawed ones—are ruled in favor of God's will, a will that irrevocably moves the people of God towards some better, brilliant future. When we see vision in this way, we and the fruits of our labor become an invincible force in living out God's decree.

THE PRESENT-DAY CRISIS OF BELIEF

The Church in the United States, and especially the urban Church, is at a crossroads of social dysfunction, cultural degradation, political gridlock, and moral neglect. Increasing unemployment, dilapidated homes, tenuous school systems, and bureaucratic inertia in government all contribute to this malaise. There is opportunity, but for the majority it is too hard to see, let alone to reach. And so people simply learn the tested art of giving up. Why not? The rich are getting richer. The middle class is shrinking, and the poor are carted off to the projects or prison or somewhere in the howling wilderness in between. Congregations either turn their backs on the crises or are powerless against them. Walking through urban centers, one cannot help but be confronted by the bitter realities of the urban archipelago, a world divided by race and class and by accent and religion, a world where some are privileged and others are pawns. It is a world of blessedness for a few but of bleakness for the many. It is a world of collision. But, I suggest, we can do something about it.

We can become the promised "city upon a hill," called by God to receive power to be witnesses, and more than that, to help our neighbor in need. We launch out on the Jericho road of present-day humanity to save our future. The problem is that many of those who belong in the community of faith do not find their existence and authority in Jesus Christ. Henry Blackaby challenges us:

> *If Christians around the world were to suddenly renounce their personal agendas, their life goals, and their aspirations, and begin responding in radical obedience to everything God showed them, the world would be turned upside down. How do we know? Because that's what first century Christians did, and the world is still talking about it.* [1]

What is needed is a conversion not in name but in witness. A metanoia—a thorough going renewal that brings us back to our first love, Jesus. We need a rendezvous with our Lord, a reunion with the power and potency of the ascension and an encounter with the Spirit that raised God's Son from the grave. This sort of encounter brings us into a place of humility and trust. Focused passion and wise service are elements that allow for the proper fruitfulness of God's work to emerge with joy. What we are in search of is a model for Church renewal that is founded upon God's principles, power, and presence. We need a Church that is deep enough to stand the storm and far reaching enough to be salt and light in the world of pain, mayhem, and misery. In short, we as a Church must be born again by the Spirit of God.

God's mission breathes dynamism, expansion, and birth. It is a holy adventure, the exhilarating drama of sheer faith. In a runaway world, God intends change: meaningful, substantive, formative change. Such change can be described as focused energy, movement towards an intended end characterized by love, peace, and justice. This is affectionately called the movement of the Spirit. From the dawn of creation God has been on a mission that propels betterment through the acts of creating, redeeming and renewing. The Church has not always been alive and awake to God's Spirit.

---

[1] Henry T. Blackaby and Richard Blackaby, Spiritual Leadership: Moving People on to God's Agenda (Nashville: B & H Publishing Group, 2011), 48.

To remain alert is part and parcel of how we wage the war of witness. Jesus tells His disciples to watch and pray. These verbs denote more action than passivity, and we must affirm work lest we fall into the rut of "do-nothingism." God says, "Behold, I am doing a new thing" (Is. 43:19). The Gospel is fresh every morning, bursting out of the arid dryness of the old and ushering into our urban centers a new season of Kingdom flourishing.

CHRIST: THE ARCHITECT OF THE VISION

The Church as the body of Christ is a sobering image. Without its connection to the head, the people who make up the Church are no more than a social tribe left to their own devices. The Church is the Lord's creation and serves as an agent of grace as it is filled with the Holy Spirit. Vision is what guides and governs our identity as we accomplish the mission and ministry of Christ through the Spirit. We must hear from God. We must adhere to His vision, for without it the community of God will perish (Prov. 29:18).

True spiritual leaders know that the vision must be made incarnate. It must speak to the pressing needs of the moment and point towards a more fulfilling future. A vision for the local urban Church that does not address the needs of the local urban community will fail to fully engage with the work of the Spirit. Vision cannot be accomplished without God. It is the future of our faith, which serves as the foundation of our fellowship. In the New Testament we have God's permission. Second Peter 1:3-4 tells us,

> *His divine power has given us everything we need for a godly life through our knowledge of Him who called us by His own glory and goodness. Through these He has given us His very great and precious promises, so that through them you may participate in the divine nature, having escaped the corruption in the world caused by evil desires.*

The vision therefore always incorporates human heads, hearts, and hands, bringing forth the requisite relationship needed to make God's will a corporate reality. The vision is not something that appears all of a sudden. Rather, it requires a period of gestation before birthing. The length of this is safeguarded and determined by God.

A Church that lacks vision is like a car without a driver. It is out of control. As a directionless machine, it is dangerous to both passengers and passersby. In time casualties will surface. When a Church loses its direction, vitality goes out the door, loyalty dissipates, and trust crumbles. The deep and abiding sense of community that once held the community together is lost.

According to Henry Blackaby,

> *The task of spiritual leadership is to move people from where they are to where God wants them to be. This is influence. Once spiritual leaders understand God's will, they make every effort to move their followers from following their own agendas to pursuing God's purposes. People who fail to move people to God's agenda have not led. They may have exhorted, cajoled, pleaded, or bullied, but they will not have led until their people have adjusted their lives to God's will.* [2]

Once spiritual leaders have done the work to understand the vision, they make every effort to move their followers from following their own ideas to pursuing God's purposes. The movement from personal agenda to God's agenda happens as people alter their attitudes and behaviours to fall in line with God's passions and patterns. Not only is the vision given by God but also the vehicle or method of corporate transformation comes from God as well. For Blackaby, only spiritual methods can be used to empower God's people to embrace God's vision. This is because spiritual leaders

---
2 Blackaby, 21.

depend on the Holy Spirit. God calls them to do something only the Holy Spirit can do.

THE CHARACTER OF VISION

No human vision is compelling enough to lead the Church. Blackaby writes: "God doesn't want people attempting to do what they think is best, but what He knows is best. No amount of reasoning and intellectualizing will discover that; God himself must reveal it."[3] God as the maker and builder of the Church is the one who must give vision, direction, and guidance. This truth is seen in 1 Corinthians, where Paul writes:

> By the grace God has given me, I laid a foundation as a wise builder, and someone else is building on it. But each one should build with care. For no one can lay any foundation other than the one already laid, which is Jesus Christ. If anyone builds on this foundation using gold, silver, costly stones, wood, hay or straw, their work will be shown for what it is, because the day will bring it to light. It will be revealed with fire, and the fire will test the quality of each person's work. If what has been built survives, the builder will receive a reward. If it is burned up, the builder will suffer loss but yet will be saved—even though only as one escaping through the flames. Don't you know that you yourselves are God's temple and that God's Spirit dwells in your midst? If anyone destroys God's temple, God will destroy that person; for God's temple is sacred, and you together are that temple. (1 Cor. 3:10-17)

Vision starts with God. It is not a human invention. It is the word made flesh. Like the Greeks who came to Nathaniel in search of our Lord, we too are driven by a compulsion to see, hear, and feel the movement of the Spirit in our lives. People who are searching for a Church to call home are looking for a Church that is pursuing and living out the vision of the Spirit of God. Vision inspires our faith. Our faith grows and is made stronger by seeing and listening with

---
3 Blackaby, 220-221.

the Spirit. By the renewing of our minds, through the enactment of vision, the Church strives to be spiritually minded in all things. "The mind governed by the flesh is death, but the mind governed by the Spirit is life and peace" (Rom. 8:6).

THE CRITERIA OF VISION

Vision must be tested and either proven or challenged in order to sift out what is worthy and meaningful from what is mere human opinion. According to James Dixon, it is important that spiritual leaders ask critical questions as they embark on capturing God's vision.[4] This task involves critical thinking and critical praying. We call it discernment. Discernment typically accompanies deliverance in the alchemy of God's grace. For Dixon, it is important that spiritual leaders ask the following pressing questions in regards to mission:

- Will it honor God?
- Will it bless people?
- Is it really needed?
- Does it require faith?

For Dixon, therefore, vision must be "a divinely inspired portrait of possibility, fueled by God's power to accomplish God's purpose, through God's people for God's praise."[5]

Vision provides value to people by serving them and asking them to serve others. Through sacrificial work and witness people become more like Christ—the one in whom we live and move and have our being. Since our being is human, vision must be humanized, enfleshed, made tangible. It may begin mysteriously, but it eventually must become expressed in concrete, intelligible form. It must show up in the lives of people in a manner in which they see themselves on the road to betterment.

---

[4] James Dixon II, If God is so Good, Why are Blacks Doing So Bad? (Charlotte: Life Bridge, Books,) 159.
[5] Ibid..

Vision calls people to bring their best selves to God and to the work of God's Kingdom. As pastors we are committed to giving God our best. The vision that we seek to implement does not represent the "best" of human planning. Rather, like the boy with two fishes and five loaves, it comes as a result of placing our heads and hearts, resources and relationships at God's disposal. In our work we believe that enthusiasm of the congregation is heightened when vision is set. The people develop trust in their leaders. To birth one's best requires the investment of time, talent, and treasure into God's Kingdom work. When this happens, it invites others to bring their best, and it attracts the attention of others.

Vision organizes and convenes the people's trust. For this to happen it must entail some very real physical and emotional components. A degree of cooperation, support, joy, and peace are essential to hearing and implementing the will of God in community. According to Peter M. Senge, "Vision spreads because of a reinforcing process of increasing clarity, enthusiasm, communication, and commitment. As people talk, the vision grows clearer. As it gets clearer, enthusiasm for its benefits builds . . . Enthusiasm can also be reinforced by early successes in pursuing the vision."[6] Roger Heuser, a professor of leadership studies, says, "The only congregations that will thrive in the coming decades will be those whose leaders have learned to respond to change, not resist it or ignore it."[7]

Since the Missio Dei is not a static program but a dynamic reality, godly leaders are called to be mentally and spiritually agile in response to the beauty, diversity, and fluidity of God's unfolding mission in the world and for the world. Here are twelve healthy habits that I have tried to adopt:

---

6 Peter M. Senge, The Fifth Discipline: The Art & Practice of The Learning Organization (New York: Currency Doubleday, 2010), 211, as cited in Roger Heuser and Norman Shawchuck, Leading The Congregation: Caring For Yourself While Serving The People (Nashville: Abingdon Press, 2010), 153-155.

7 Roger Heuser and Norman Shawchuck, Leading The Congregation: Caring For Yourself While Serving The People (Nashville: Abingdon Press, 2010), 176.

1. Study the lives of great biblical leaders, great leaders in the Church, and great leaders of history.

2. Initiate and develop social, cultural, and technological awareness forums within the congregation.

3. Eagerly seek out and engage people with constructive thoughts, creative imaginations, and compassionate spirits.

4. Develop an attitude of learning.

5. Become a friend of social media and technology.

6. Set aside time to encounter new ideas through travel, YouTube, and coursework in other fields.

7. Develop an area of interest outside of the pulpit. Be open to new experiences and developments.

8. Take excursions through nature.

9. Be self-aware: understand your own passions, preferences, pressure points, limitations, biases, and prejudgments.

10. Develop listening pools, brainstorming sessions, and small group study cells.

11. Take a course or learn a new craft.

12. Cultivate relationships with people that represent different ethnic backgrounds, social experiences, mental outlooks, language systems, and intellectual traditions.

Vision is like an artist painting a landscape. The landscape exists outside the painter, thus providing the visual picture of what the artist will translate on canvas. The painter does not create the landscape. It is simply presented to him. His task is to capture the essence of the landscape first in his mind and then for a different medium. The same holds true for anyone who seeks to birth a new reality, such as a photographer or an architect—or a Church leader. God is the creator of our vision; it is up to us to grasp it and implement it.

CHAPTER FIVE

NOT BY POWER, NOR BY MIGHT:

SPIRITUAL WARFARE AND COMPASSION

Spiritual combat is another element of life which needs to be taught anew and proposed once more to all Christians today. It is a secret and interior art, an invisible struggle in which [we] engage every day against the temptations, the evil suggestions that the demon tries to plant in [our] hearts.
—Pope John Paul II

He who does not believe in the devil does not believe in the Gospel.
—Pope John Paul II

For our struggle is not against flesh and blood, but against the rulers, against the authorities, against the powers of this dark world and against the spiritual forces of evil in the heavenly realms.
—Eph. 6:12

How do pastors help their congregations navigate human wickedness?

Compassion is at the heart of the Church's divine errand. The suffering that compassion eradicates often (but not always) results from human finitude and frailty. I propose that we become compassionate warriors in order to address the systematic sin at work in our urban communities. The compassionate warrior seeks to intervene against evil on behalf of Christ and His Church. The New Testament witness forcefully declares that the reign of God has its enemies, and as a result, compassionate ministry must guard against those forces that would dilute its missional potency (Rom. 8:37-39; 2 Cor. 10:4-5; Eph. 6:10-11; 2 Thes. 3:3; 1 Pet. 5:8-9). The compassionate warrior, then, is called to engage in spiritual warfare.

Immediately after Peter discloses Jesus' divine identity, Jesus makes the remarkable claim that He will build His Church upon "this rock" (Peter) and that His Church will be impregnable against the gates of hell. Jesus is saying that He is going to build a glorious reality upon an imperfect human foundation. He says further to Peter, "I will give you the keys to the kingdom" (Mt. 16:19). Keys open and lock doors. They suggest that a certain space is accessible to a specific person, select group, or a specific community—but not to all. Jesus' instructions to Peter suggest that not everyone has access to certain powers, places, and privileges in the Kingdom. The ability to do mighty works is the provenance of those like Simon Peter who understand Christ's lordship over all history and creation.

Following Peter, we as Christ's disciples are called and charged to be stewards of certain gifts, talents, and abilities. As such, we will provide an account of our stewardship to God. God's Kingdom exists in a perpetual state of warfare, and the compassionate steward engages in combat as a witness and seal of the reign of God. If we are to follow where the Spirit leads, we are left with no choice but to be permanently prepared for battle.

Spiritual warfare involves four identifiable components:

1. Supplication
2. Sight
3. Standing
4. Strategizing

SUPPLICATION

Supplication is the first stage of warfare. It is the principal mechanism by which the Church of Jesus Christ remains alive to the Spirit. Without the Spirit we are left bereft of the truth, which is our oxygen. Prayer is the process by which we negotiate and overcome moral and spiritual evil, the death-dealing forces of the cosmos. St. Louis de Montfort tells us, "Pray with great confidence, with confidence based upon the goodness and infinite generosity of God and upon the promises of Jesus Christ. God is a spring of living water which flows unceasingly into the hearts of those who pray." Isaiah warns the people of Israel about their failure to seek the Lord:

> *Woe to those who go down to Egypt for help, who rely on horses, who trust in the multitude of their chariots and in the great strength of their horsemen, but do not look to the Holy One of Israel, or seek help from the LORD. Yet he too is wise and can bring disaster; he does not take back his words. He will rise up against that wicked nation, against those who help evildoers. But the Egyptians are mere mortals and not God; their horses are flesh and not spirit. When the LORD stretches out his hand, those who help will stumble, those who are helped will fall; all will perish together. (Is. 31:1-3)*

Prayer in spiritual warfare is always aimed at some specific action, and so the second aspect of such warfare is seeing clearly.

SIGHT

> *My son, do not let wisdom and understanding out of your sight, preserve sound judgment and discretion. (Prov. 3:21)*

The compassionate warrior sees God, self, and the world through spiritual eyes. "Open my eyes that I may see wonderful things in your law," says the Psalmist (Ps. 119:18). We embrace God's wisdom as we attempt to discern the real source and structure of evil. Our wisdom, like grace, lies outside ourselves and is supplied by the Spirit. Yet we reflect godly wisdom in the ways in which we pattern our lives after Christ. Critical and earnest study of God's word is indispensable for an understanding of the complex and clandestine ways in which evil works itself into the systems of this world and into the structure of our lives. A.W. Tozer said,

> *Among the gifts of the Spirit, scarcely is one of greater practical usefulness than the gift of discernment. This gift should be highly valued and frankly sought as being almost indispensable in these critical times. This gift will enable us to distinguish the chaff from the wheat and to divide the manifestations of the flesh from the operations of the Spirit.* [1]

For the compassionate warrior, warfare is a many-headed monster. Every phase and forum of the believer's life is wrought with unexpected challenges. Faith, grounded in the biblical story, is how we navigate those challenges. Our ability to map progress grows as we acquire the inspiration and insight that come by absorbing biblical truths. Life in the Spirit is the only insurance against the calamity of human wisdom.

---

[1] A. W. Tozer, as quoted in Men Sharpen Men, "What is Spiritual Discernment." www.men-sharpen-men.org/2004-09-17_Discernment1.doc.

The Holy Spirit comprehends the perfect will and indubitable thoughts of the Father and reveals them to the Church. Jesus said, "Blessed are the pure in heart, for they shall see God" (Mt. 5:8). The will of God is our promise and our permission to live victoriously through the Spirit in the midst of ceaseless opposition and endless strife (John 14:16-17; 16:13; 1 Cor. 2:10-12).

Jesus Christ is "wisdom from God" (1 Cor. 1:30). Therefore wisdom, the ability to feel, think, and live with and through the Spirit, is birthed and animated by our passionate acknowledgement of the Lordship of Jesus Christ (James 1:5; Phil. 1:9). The world cannot provide the wisdom that comes from God. We become educated in the ways of God only as we yield the desires of our hearts to the will of God. Within this act of sheer grace lies the sublime quest of the psalmist, "Teach me knowledge and good judgment, for I trust your commands" (Ps. 119:66). The wisdom that comes from growing in Christ is not simply a change of worldview or reversal of social perspective. It is a fundamental reorientation of one's being towards God. Spiritual sight is the product of a buoyant faith that initiates obedience. "Without faith it is impossible to please God" (Hebrews 11:16). While we may derive value through academic pursuit and professional competence, ultimately we are only able to please God through the purification of our beliefs and behavior, a goal that is met by a deeper knowledge of God's intentions. Our walk with Jesus begins as an act of revelation and is further developed through prayer, simplicity, and meditation (Heb. 5:14; Phil. 1:9).

As we grow through this tumultuous drama of joy and pain, hope and despair, we bear the fruit of wisdom. The Holy Spirit reveals truths about these emotions, allowing us to bear fruit worthy of Christ. The heart of spiritual vision is the capacity to distinguish the will and heart of God from the ways of humans or from Satan. Sight can only come by obedience. "The Spirit of the Lord will rest upon the one who obeys—the Spirit of wisdom and of understanding, the Spirit of counsel and of power, the Spirit of knowledge and of the fear of the Lord. The one who obeys will not judge by what is seen with eyes, or decide by what is heard with ears" (Is. 11:2-3).

The quest to navigate this warfare can only rightfully be undertaken in Christian community. No single believer is equipped with sufficient spiritual sight to escape the traps of the evil one. In Christian community we gain the humility, discernment, diligence, stamina, and patience necessary for basic training in the conduct of spiritual warfare. Christ only is our "blessed assurance." "Through Him alone do we have access to one another, joy in one another, and fellowship with one another."[2] Constant attention to "the inner sanctuary" is more powerfully conducted when one is a part of a living community of faith where creativity, accountability, and responsibility to grow are seen as prerequisites for Christian discipleship. These elements, which are formed and strengthened through friendships, families, and congregations, are indispensable to engage the complex campaign of warfare. There is a considerable difference in how a solitary person may combat evil and how a community of saints may be mobilized to fight the adversary. We must have eyes on the ways in which Satan seeks to destroy not only God's Church but all of humankind as children of God. The Christian must see through the eyes of the Spirit. This allows the Christian to live in spite of fear—not removing fear, but transcending it and displacing it. In its place is the courage to be. This courage is found in community.

STANDING

To be a Christian is to be on trial, constantly haunted and harassed. The enemy perennially accuses the believer of sin. As witnesses of Christ we operate with the boldness of the New Testament faith.

---

[2] Dietrich Bonhoeffer, Life Together (New York: HarperOne, 2009), 39.

Being alert, aware, and alive in the Spirit powers our missional stance. "Beloved, do not believe every spirit, but test the spirits to see whether they are from God, for many false prophets have gone out into the world" (I John 4:1). Courage is indispensable for spiritual warfare. Courage is the capacity to take risks in the face of significant odds.

El Salvadorian Archbishop Oscar Romero spent the last years of his life sacrificing for the poor who were being routinely persecuted, tortured, slaughtered and who "disappeared." This often occurred with the approval of state authorities and was ignored by many in the Church. Days before his brutal murder, Romero told a reporter, "You can tell the people that if they succeed in killing me, that I forgive and bless those who do it. Hopefully, they will realize they are wasting their time. A bishop will die, but the Church of God, which is the people, will never perish."[3] Furthermore, Romero was highly critical of those ministers of the Gospel who embraced the status quo. In the face of governmental barbarities, these ministers offered homilies of comfort and quietism rather than challenging their congregations to embrace the rewarding hardship that comes by way of bearing one's cross.

> *A Church that suffers no persecution but enjoys the privileges and support of the things of the earth—beware!—is not the true Church of Jesus Christ. A preaching that does not point out sin is not the preaching of the Gospel. A preaching that makes sinners feel good, so that they are secured in their sinful state, betrays the Gospel's call.* [4]

Father Oscar Romero is a gallant example of a courageous spiritual warrior, a spiritual agent unafraid to live from the center of his spiritual being, refusing the easy path of psychological or moral escapism. His life and words show that without embracing the

---
[3] Oscar Romero, http://www.uscatholic.org/culture/social-justice/2009/02/oscar-romero-bishop-poor.
[4] Oscar Romero, The Violence of Love (Orbis Books, 2004), 125.

work of self-purification, one's inner demons gain the upper hand in spiritual warfare, rendering us unwittingly vulnerable and prone to become drafted to the wrong side of the conflict. That is why courage signals the believer's call to conscience and to face the enemies. One must be willing to brace oneself against the awful blast of rejection and ostracism, even hate, and still stand. To stand face to face with ghastly terror is something that is not possible within the shell of carnal humanity. One needs the Spirit.

Courage is an invitation to death. The grain must first fall to the ground in order to yield fruit. Without being imbedded, the grain remains dormant and is unable to unlock its inner potential and extend life. The death and burial of our own selfish inclinations is the seed of the harvest of God's intentions for humanity. Through this we arrive at a deeper meaning of God's purpose. The death to self is a death to blindness. Now we "see" in order to know how to stand, to avoid Satan's trap, to "fight the good fight," to live. Paul Tillich said,

> *The courage to be is the ethical act in which man affirms his own being in spite of those elements of his existence which conflict with his essential self-affirmation . . . It is the affirmation of one's essential nature, one's inner aim or entelechy (vital force, realization), but it is an affirmation which has in itself the character of "in spite of."* [5]

STRATEGIZING

Finding the courage to stand is not enough. To prevail in spiritual warfare one must develop a strategy to defeat the enemy. Prayer, waiting, listening, thinking, and organizing are essential tools in the campaign against the adversary. Great visionaries of faith have often been great strategists. Nehemiah, a sterling example of

---

5 Paul Tillich, The Courage to Be (New Haven: Yale University Press, 2000), 3-4.

visionary organizational leadership, developed an action plan to rebuild the Jerusalem wall. God honored his prayerful planning.

NEHEMIAH: A MODEL FOR THE CHURCH

It is evident from the first chapter of Nehemiah that he invested much time in prayer. His prayer informed the strategic planning that framed his sophisticated approach to the king, his prudent gathering of resources en route to Jerusalem, his inspection of the city that lay in ruin, his selection of key leaders, and his organization and equipping of the builders. He earnestly sought God's face long before he made his petition known to the king. "Planning that arises from and is the product of prayer is far superior to planning that is merely backed by prayer."[6] Proverbs 3:5-6 puts it this way: "Trust in the LORD with all your heart; and lean not on your own understanding. In all your ways submit to Him, and He will make your paths straight."

Nehemiah believed in his heart that it was God's will for the wall of Jerusalem to be rebuilt. He gladly embraced the central role God had called him to play in national and civic rehabilitation. However, he did not rush into action. Before undertaking such a colossal assignment, Nehemiah strategized. He formulated a practical plan of action to meet the challenge of rebuilding the walls. Nehemiah was successful because he coupled heartfelt prayer with careful and creative planning. The biblical witness warns against the folly of engaging spiritual warfare without a defensible plan of direction and execution.

> *Suppose a king is about to go to war against another king. Won't he first sit down and consider whether he is able with ten thousand men to oppose the one coming against him with twenty thousand? (Luke 14:31)*

---

[6] John White, Excellence in Leadership: Reaching Goals with Prayer, Leadership, and Determination (Downer's Grove, IL: InterVarsity Press, 1986), 40.

The person without the Spirit does not accept the things that come from the Spirit of God but considers them foolishness, and cannot understand them because they are discerned only through the Spirit. (I Cor. 2:14)

STRATEGY IN SPIRITUAL WARFARE

Strategy in spiritual warfare involves the planning and execution of the never-ending contest that exists between the children of light and the children of darkness. The compassionate warrior does not use physical force so much as the robust faith of head and heart to accomplish his or her assignment. Strategy, which is a subdiscipline of warfare, drives the mission of the Church against the kingdom of darkness. Faith engenders and enables strategy by providing the required creative intelligence. Typically, in military campaigns, troops engaged in warfare must gain territory or at least expand their influence on the field of battle. Discipleship, which is the gridiron of mission, channels the process by which the Church gains vital moral ground against the forces of darkness and ushers in the Kingdom of God. The result is that human life turns back to God. Human systems are realigned with their original purposes. Salvation, which is the goal of all creation, is no longer mere theory but a real, lived out, faithful anticipation of a future full of peace, a future where the lion and the lamb lie down together. Strategy pilots the Church's mission and addresses the question of how a single Christian, a particular congregation, or a denomination of the universal Church is to carry out its mission given a particular set of circumstances or series of obstacles and specific challenges.

Derived from the Greek, strategy (**Greek "strategia"**) means the art of developing and deploying troops or personnel. It involves equipping, training, and execution; planning and conduct of campaigns; and the movement and disposition of forces. It also connotes team conduct or the concept of operational dynamics.

The Church of Jesus Christ has always sought to form and reform itself to meet the challenges of changing circumstances. For the Christian, the Bible constitutes the first and last word on spiritual warfare. As in armed military strategy, spiritual warfare involves using available resources such as people, equipment, and information against the opponent's resources to gain supremacy or subdue the opponent. All spiritual warfare is governed by Jesus, whose commandment, "Make disciples of all nations, baptizing them in the name of the Father, Son and the Holy Spirit" (Mt. 28:19), enlists human participation in Christ's redeeming work to all humanity.

In light of this commandment, the above military analogy is apt only up to a point. For the Christian warrior does not use swords or shields, guns or grenades. The aim of all Christian spiritual warfare is peace. The Church enters believing that Christ is our peace and has, through the crucifixion, broken down the barriers that separate us from God and from one another (Eph. 2:14-16). The primary weapons are the spiritual disciplines, such as fasting, solitude, and simplicity. Paul says as well,

> *The weapons we fight with are not the weapons of the world. On the contrary, they have divine power to demolish strongholds. We demolish arguments and every pretension that sets itself up against the knowledge of God, and we take captive every thought to make it obedient to Christ. And we will be ready to punish every act of disobedience, once your obedience is complete. (2 Cor. 10:4-5)*

In spiritual warfare the first enemy of the compassionate soldier is the self. It is only by conquering the enemy that is our own carnality that we learn the discipline to grow in faith, seeking the revelation of God's strategy against the decrees of this world. When he or she has conquered self, then the soldier is empowered to fight off the life-denying forces of sin and evil that grip individuals, ideas, and institutions.

The work of exposing the schemes and strategies of the enemy is key to the development of a formidable war campaign that constitutes the groundwork for the victorious life. Believers must know that in Christ they have been given the keys to the Kingdom; that they not only possess the ability and the authority to wage war but have been given the final victory over the adversary. This cumbersome and complex task can only be performed under the authority of Jesus. This topsy-turvy, tension-charged affair is highlighted in the classic parable of the wheat and the tares, to which we will now turn.

THE PARABLE OF THE WHEAT AND THE TARES

The world of early Rome was no stranger to the pervasive presence of sickness and disease, demonic possession, witchcraft, and systemic and corporate exclusion. Private and public life were filled with threat, tension, and tragedy. The life of a poor Galilean was constantly imperiled by the massive incursion of cultural and political forces. Many of those who followed the Master's teaching were social nobodies, a motley group of alienated humanity. Compounding their misery was the severe economic deprivation that rendered them invisible. It is no wonder that Jesus constantly prepared His disciples to deal with the permanent and extensive reality of evil. His pedagogy regarding ushering in the Kingdom of God included supplying His followers with tools for overcoming the real and complex enemy. No doubt there were times in which His disciples felt anxiety-ridden, overwhelmed, perturbed, and forlorn. After all, they were a subjugated people, a belittled minority—"wrong seemed to be forever on the throne,"[7] to use James Russell Lowell's fitting line.

---

7 James Russell Lowell, "The Present Crisis," Academy of American Poets, http://www.poets.org/poetsorg/poem/present-crisis

Yet Jesus was ever hopeful. He used this hope to point out that evil, no matter how potent and constant, would never totally subdue the Kingdom of Heaven. The parable of the wheat and the tares is used to illustrate the reality of evil in tension with the ever-loving presence of God.

> *The kingdom of heaven is like a man who sowed good seed in his field. But while everyone was sleeping, his enemy came and sowed weeds among the wheat, and went away. When the wheat sprouted and formed heads, then the weeds also appeared. The owner's servants came to him and said, "Sir, didn't you sow good seed in your field? Where then did the weeds come from?" "An enemy did this" he replied. The servants asked him, "Do you want us to go and pull them up?" "No," he answered, "because while you are pulling weeds, you may uproot the wheat with them. Let both grow together until the harvest. At that time I will tell the harvesters: First collect the weeds and tie them in bundles to be burned; then gather the wheat and bring it to my barn."'* (Mt. 13:24-30)

Jesus uses the parable to illustrate the reality of oppositional forces, spiritual combat, and the power of God to overcome the forces of evil. First-century Jews were often victims of national political domination. Jesus' selection of agricultural imagery conveys much to His contemporaries. The one who sowed the seeds is the Son of Man, Jesus Christ Himself. It is Jesus who has the Kingdom. We are His workers and servants, the Church. The field is the world, the community of human beings. The aim is to bring forth a good crop, the ekklesia, the radical community of new, vibrant believers—the Church of Jesus Christ. We are called out of the world to engage it and transform it. The good seed symbolizes those Christians who grow and flourish into Christian maturity. The Church as the righteous Kingdom is called to maintain its purity and its fidelity to the Gospel of Jesus Christ. In this way it builds and maintains a community of righteousness and holiness (1 Pet. 1:15-16, 2:9-10, 1 John 2:1).

Those in Jesus' immediate audience know weeds imperil the wheat, thereby wasting the good energy of the farmer and limiting the chances of a good harvest. No doubt many of them were familiar with the practice of some farmers to sabotage the crops of others and thereby reduce competition. Furthermore, these weeds were sown under the clandestine garment of night, indicating a harmful intent. Even more portentously, weeds appear only after the wheat has sprouted. As soon as the crop shows signs of life and strength, the weeds come to destroy. Not only are weeds unpleasant and uncontrollable, they are also unappealing to the eye. There are likewise persons or practices that choke life out of the believer, leaving them spiritually languid and listless, draining them of the creativity and vitality needed to live lives of spiritual productivity and moral potency.

We are to stand guard against this enemy (Eph. 6). The weeds are the source of the world's diseases, rebellion, and confusion. They are enemies to the productivity, fertility, and creativity of God's reign—the work of the Spirit. Yet we are to engage the enemy in the most peculiar way, in a way that is senseless to a world riveted on violence, mayhem, and revenge. It is the warring of relentless nonviolent love. Oscar Romero says,

> *We have never preached violence, except the violence of love, which left Christ nailed to a cross, the violence that we must each do to ourselves to overcome our selfishness and such cruel inequalities among us. The violence we preach is not the violence of the sword, the violence of hatred. It is the violence of love, of brotherhood, the violence that wills to beat weapons into sickles for work.*[8]

The enemy comes to sow seeds of division, dissension, and destruction. The compassionate warrior is the one who sows the

---

8 Romero, The Violence of Love (Farmington, PA: Plough Publishing House, 1998), v.

good seed, anticipating the consummation of God's salvific activity. Wickedness and evil are constant thorns in the side of servants of the King. Violence and vice constantly bombard the lives of followers of Christ, causing many to lose hope to the point that they feel morally worthless. The compassionate warrior must be alert and believe that the ultimate aim of the Eternal God is to bring the Kingdom seed to full harvest.

First, the compassionate warrior must understand that we must seek God through prayer to have the discernment and wisdom to both identify the "weeds" and to know how to respond to them. "Weeds" can so resemble the "wheat" that it is hard to distinguish between the two, especially at the early stages of their grown. At times, the wheat and weeds grow so close together that to cut one is to cut the other. We see this lived out in the life of Jesus himself, a life practice we are called to imitate.

Jesus Christ lived in the midst of His enemies. At the end all His disciples deserted him. On the cross, He was utterly alone, surrounded by evildoers and mockers. For this cause He had come, to bring peace to the enemies of God. So the Christian, too, belongs not in the seclusion of a cloistered life but in the thick of foes. There is his commission, his work.

> *"The kingdom is to be in the midst of your enemies. And he who will not suffer this does not want to be of the Kingdom of Christ; he wants to be among friends, to sit among roses and lilies, not with the bad people but the devout people. O you blasphemers and betrayers of Christ! If Christ had done what you are doing who would ever have been spared."* [9]

It is important to note that the owner issues a stern caution to his workers: "Let both grow together." The desire of the owner,

---

9 Dietrich Bonhoeffer, Life Together (New York: HarperOne, 2009), 17.

who understands what his crops need for healthy growth, is not to eliminate the weeds. Jesus hints that the weeds have a purpose. In their effort to wreak havoc, the weeds actually promote the growth of the wheat. The mystery of the parable is contained in the odd premise that wheat gains resilience and resourcefulness by having to struggle with the weeds for life's essentials.

Herein lies the mystery of the logic of the Kingdom of God. Struggle is a prerequisite for growth. Weeds fuel the growth of wheat. Evil in some mysterious way adds to the development of good. To be sure, plants need water, air, sunlight, and other nutrients to grow. This process is called photosynthesis. Yet there is more. The wheat is so precious to the owner that he does not want it to be mistakenly gathered up with the weeds. To expel the wheat along with the weeds is to equate the two. Jesus is making it clear that the value of wheat is infinitely superior to that of weeds.

There is an ethical warning here that cannot be ignored. Jesus is pushing for caution. A hurried response on behalf of the workers may wreak negative consequences. The owner embodies patience, whereas the workers desire immediate redress. Therein lies the gulf between the two parties—and between the believer and a gracious God. The urge of the workers to handle business mirrors the attitude of many Christians whose behavior lacks compassion, prudence, and longsuffering. It is not uncommon for people to take justice into their own hands, to deal with opposition forthrightly and with immediate alacrity. Yet what may be fair and righteous on the surface may turn out to conceal trouble. In our human lens we often err in judgment. This expressed arrogance wrongfully shapes the outlook of many contemporary leaders and congregants. For justice too often looks like intolerance and exclusion of people who carry differences other than our own. The quest of the compassionate warrior is to wage warfare against spiritual wickedness but not send people to hell. To stand against wickedness is to wage warfare against spiritual wickedness but not send people to hell. To stand against wickedness is to work for justice without carrying and spreading the seed of bitterness. Public fairness requires private virtue. Spiritual awareness includes thorough self-examination, without which we cannot be apostles of love and angels of light.

PART TWO

THE DAMASCUS ENCOUNTER: IN SEARCH OF THE GODLY CITY

Now the American city has been transformed. The poor still inhabit the miserable housing in the central area, but they are increasingly isolated from contact with, or sight of, anybody else. Middle-class women coming in from Suburbia on a rare trip may catch the merest glimpse of the other America on the way to an evening at the theater, but the children are segregated in suburban schools. The business or professional man may drive along the fringes of slums in a car or bus, but it is not an important experience to him. The failure, the unskilled, the disabled, the aged, and the minorities are right there, across the tracks, where they have always been. But hardly anyone else is.

—Michael Harrington, *The Other America*

A human being is a part of the whole called by us universe, a part limited in time and space. He experiences himself, his thoughts and feelings as something separated from the rest, a kind of optical delusion of his consciousness. This delusion is a kind of

prison for us, restricting us to our personal desires and to affection for a few persons nearest to us. Our task must be to free ourselves from this prison by widening our circle of compassion to embrace all living creatures and the whole of nature in its beauty.
—Albert Einstein

We who lived in concentration camps can remember the men who walked through the huts comforting others, giving away their last piece of bread. They may have been few in number, but they offer sufficient proof that everything can be taken from a man but one thing: the last of the human freedoms—to choose one's attitude in any given set of circumstances, to choose one's own way.
—Viktor Frankl

How far you go in life depends on your being tender with the young, compassionate with the aged, sympathetic with the striving and tolerant of the weak and strong. Because someday in life you will have been all of these.
—George Washington Carver

Contemporary urban America, with its mix of ethnicities, economics, and ethics, presents a unique set of challenges to communities of faith that once thrived with energy, enlightenment, creativity, and commitment. We now find these qualities dying on the vine of social malaise. This daunting reality strangles our corporate creativity, leaving us half dead on the Jericho road of modern America. In the words of Matthew Arnold, it is as if an old world is dying and a new world is powerless to be born.

Johnny Ray Youngblood, a pioneer in transformational urban leadership, is fond of saying that the cemetery is a great place to have resurrections. The Church has at times provided the moral bedrock of life. Given the changing nature of the family and tenuous character of the public education system that warehouses so much of our young people's moral and creative potential, the Church remains the last place of hope and solidarity. While home and school are suffering from a severe lack of resources and relationships, the Church remains the most sustainable vehicle for community empowerment and social regeneration, especially in marginalized communities.

There has always been an intimate relationship between the Church and educational institutions. The social authority of the Church helps to shape the web of values, feelings, moods, and practices in urban communities. Yet the era in which the Christian Church was the defining authority in the United States has come and gone. We have entered a period of ideological pluralism, and urban areas are particularly affected by a multiplicity of views. The gargantuan changes in technology, including communications, and the shifting of jobs overseas and to the suburbs have combined to reduce the availability of jobs. The result of increased unemployment is community instability, poor schooling, limited opportunities for entrepreneurship, and a weak political unity. Absentee parenthood, the deluge of drugs, the widening gap between rich and poor, and the rise of a prison-industrial complex are all problems common to urban communities.

Hence, due to the precipitous decline in quality of social and economic services, urban dwellers have fewer safeguards from the ravages of insensitive and even reckless governmental policies, predatory economic scams, and multi-national corporate intrusions. William Julius Wilson has famously argued that there is a negative correlation between joblessness and social organization in urban ghettos. As Wilson writes, "Neighborhoods plagued with high levels of joblessness are more likely to experience low levels of social organization; the two go hand in hand. High rates of joblessness trigger other neighborhood problems that undermine social organization, ranging from crime, gang violence, and drug trafficking to family breakups and problems in the organization of family life."[1] Many of these people feel that their lives do not make a difference—and they have felt so for many decades.

After the significant, and in some ways Herculean, efforts of the 1960s to close the income gap between rich and poor Americans and raise the quality of life for a substantial slice of the U.S., many urban spaces came under siege. Hence, urban dwellers, many of whom made up the upwardly mobile middle class, fled to the bucolic suburbs, initiating the exodus of numerous social services and viable economic institutions. This accelerated the decline and decay of the once respectable communities. The consequence is distress and emotional despair that has ultimately led to defeat. Lacking the requisite intellectual and social capital, many urban dwellers live and labor on the margins of civil society, ultimately falling through the cracks to become part of the systems that plague urban communities.

None of this means, of course, that urban dwellers lack the creative and constructive skills or the moral fervor to succeed. It simply means that the context of their lives presents challenges that Churches should be aware of and actively seek to offer the life-giving power of the resurrected Christ.

---

[1] William Julius Williams, When Work Disappears: The World of the New Urban Poor (New York: Random House, 1997), 21.

CHAPTER SIX

A HOLE IN MY SOUL:

NIHILISM AND THE CHURCH

Shame is a soul-eating emotion.
　　　—Carl Jung

I see in the fight club the strongest and smartest men who've ever lived. I see all this potential and I see squandering. God damn it, an entire generation pumping gas, waiting tables, slaves with white collars, advertising has us chasing cars and clothes, working jobs we hate so we can buy shit we don't need. We're the middle children of the history of man, no purpose or place, we have no Great war, no Great depression, our great war is a spiritual war, our great depression is our lives, we've been all raised by television to believe that one day we'd all be millionaires and movie gods and rock stars, but we won't and we're slowly learning that fact. And we're very, very pissed off.
　　　—Chuck Palahniuk, Fight Club

We live in an age of anomie. Our religion of relativism bows at the twin altars of aggressive individualism and egoistic hedonism. From the rooftops of politics and popular culture we hear the single refrain: I alone count—nothing is worth pursuing. In a culture that expresses little respect for moral devotions and civic loyalties, it is not surprising that reported cases of mental illness and depression are so pervasive. The fragility of the human spirit requires devotion to a moral and psychic reality that can sift through its nagging questions. The current climate of depression can be read as the patent human response to the absence of the vital resources that enlist human commitment and help persons navigate the riddles of existence. If nihilism implies the absence of a canopy of meaning, the insufficiency of responses to the human quest for meaning, then depression means that persons simply don't know where to begin. It means the soul has ceased the act of searching, which is the one thing the soul must do to be satisfied. Depression says: everything I have given my life to has failed. Therefore I refuse to give my life anymore. Nihilism and depression are two sides of the same existential coin.

NIHILISM IN FOCUS

The monumental fraying of the social webs that once provided a healthy sense of community for so many Americans has contributed to the pathetic lack of civility and individuality that feeds the thick cultural malaise in so many pockets of American life. The profound sense of desperation and gnawing helplessness eats away at the body, setting up the conditions for anarchic potential. Many Americans are simply surrendering the struggle of life. A society that promises the moon and leaves its denizens dashed against the rocks of broken dreams is a society in which anarchy looms. Dreams deferred often explode. No wonder then that our city streets are swelling with anger. Young and old feel tortured, unfulfilled, empty, and hollow—pressed against the wall. This heavy unease, the increase in the numbers of at-risk youth, families, and elderly in communities that lack credible access to the ideas and resources that provide a way out of this unease, contributes to what Mark

Taylor has aptly called "Lockdown America"[1] —a feeling that we are caged and shackled. A sense that we are doomed from within and without. A sense that we have no voice, no agency, and that the world we live in is "like a jungle sometimes, it makes me wonder how [we] keep from going under."[2]

The pervasive mood that whatever I do I will not make a difference only fuels our desperation. In part we feel hopeless because the idols that we erected in our world of fantasy are ill equipped to support us against the standard miseries of existence. I feel irrelevant, and I have a profound sense that whatever gesture I make towards self-improvement or the common good will amount to nothing. The current platforms of cultural expression often fuel a hyper-materialism, the notion that what I own defines me, and so therefore the more I own the bigger I am.

A young D.C. native expressing such hopelessness says, "I am not a basketball player. I am not supermodel. So what is left?" In her world the exploitation of the body and not the exploration of the world leads to success. With standard corridors of education closed to her, who can blame her that she only sees the cauldron of a misery enveloping her?

Thomas Hibbs[3] describes nihilism as a state of spiritual impoverishment in which the boundaries between right and wrong, value and meaninglessness, worth and waste are eclipsed. Nihilism makes us feel that we have a hole in our soul. Under such conditions despair rocks us to sleep in the midst of a war zone, a war of annihilation in which we see no ultimate purpose. We lose the why of our existence, and these shrunken aspirations make it

---

1 Mark Lewis Taylor, The Executed God: The Way of the Cross in Lockdown America (Minneapolis: Augsburg Fortress, 2001).
2 A line from Grand Master Flash's hip hop classic, "The Message."
3 Thomas S. Hibbs, Shows About Nothing: Nihilism in the Popular Culture (Baylor, TX: Baylor University Press, 2012).

hard to differentiate between immediate gratification and long-term results.

NIHILISM, DEPRESSION AND THE CHURCH

The nihilistic poisons that pervade so much of urban America find their way into the pews and pulpits of Christ's Church. Congregants of all theological orientations and backgrounds are torn and tattered by the two-headed beast of nihilism and cynicism. Congregational depression, caused by varying levels and combinations of grief, loss and anxiety, confines much of the institutional Christian witness in North America to bondage.

Mark Mounts, a pastor and licensed professional counselor, has this to say about the scourge of depression:

> I'm still a pastor, but now I'm also a professional counselor and therapist, and my years of professional experience have shown me that depression is far from unique among Christians. Many pastors and parishioners feel that no matter how much they get involved and how much time they sacrifice, they just can't shed the gloominess that seems to follow them everywhere. So they work harder and give more with the hope that this will make the gloom go away. They try Bible study, but they can't seem to focus. They try prayer, but they don't know what to say. Even worse, they don't feel like being around people anymore, whether at Church or at home. They're not as patient as they used to be. They get frustrated and angry more easily. Little things that never used to bother them now do. And guilt sets in; they get angry at themselves, try to set new schedules and goals to make themselves do what they know they should, only to be disappointed at their seemingly endless lack of "character" to follow through. Their

tempers get shorter and shorter, or they escape to the isolation of their beds, not having the energy toeven start the day.[4]

DEPRESSION AND DYSFUNCTIONAL CONGREGATIONS

Jesus told us there would be conflict: "I have told you these things, so that in me you may have peace. In this world you will have trouble. But take heart! I have overcome the world" (John 16:33). When depression is left unchecked it can quickly develop into rage. Anger is not sin. In fact anger may be a healthy response towards a particularly negative or hurtful experience. Seen positively, anger is a natural and key feature of the human experience. The human capacity to feel anger may push us to achieve the goals of justice, peacemaking, and righteousness. In this sense it serves as an index for morality, distinguishing between right and wrong, good and evil. Leroy Howe argues that anger is gift from God.[5] Anger sensitizes us toward both the will of God and the suffering of humankind. Because we are creatures made in His image and after His likeness, anger is part of the divine human make up. "For the wrath of God is revealed from heaven against all ungodliness and unrighteousness of men, who suppress the truth in unrighteousness" (Rom. 1:18).[6]

Yet before we press this point too far we must acknowledge that humans share God's anger but in radically distinct ways. God's anger is a product of divine love and grace. Our anger oftentimes is mixed up with fleshly desires and selfish ambitions. Uncontrolled anger or blind rage can be potentially destructive to the life of the individual person as well as the bonds of the community of faith.

---

[4] Mark Mounts has a Masters in Professional Counseling from Liberty University and is a Licensed Professional Counselor in the Houston area. Mark did his pre-graduate internship at Texas Children's Hospital in Houston and focused in the area of Early Childhood Intervention. Mark now has a part-time counseling practice at the Houston Center for Christian Counseling where he counsels children, teens, families, and individual adults. He is also a full-time pastor for Community Christian Fellowship (a congregation of Grace Communion International). http://www.gci.org/CO/depression
[5] See his important work, Angry People in the Pews (Valley Forge: Judson Press, 2001).
[6] See also Ps. 78:56-66; Deut. 1:26-46; Josh. 7:1; Ps. 2:1-6; Zeph. 1:14-15; Luke 16:19-31.

Congregations have been held hostage by explosive and lethal public outbursts of anger, shut-outs, withheld pledges, and even lawsuits. Earlier we spoke about spiritual warfare. Depression is an enemy of the soul working against the Spirit of Christ in order to hijack the witness of the Church. Depression is a form of anger. Depressed people feel justified in injuring others. They become blind to their own hang-ups and suffocate the will to reconcile. People who are angry feel abandoned and isolated. They have no mental place of reference, and the symbols that once provided inspiration and a sense of purpose no longer mean anything. Persons who have progressed to this stage of depression tend to blame others for their mistakes. They may be mistrustful of order and seek ways to undermine authority, resenting pastoral authority in general and the word of God specifically. They deny the power of God.

> *Antagonists are individuals who, on the basis of nonsubstantive evidence, go out of their way to make insatiable demands, usually attacking the person or performance of others. These attacks are selfish in nature, tearing down rather than building up, and are often directed against those in a leadership capacity.*[7]

Hugh Halverstadt argues that Church conflict does not have to degenerate into nihilism, into a hopeless war of all against all.[8] People with strong and differing views can still receive and adopt the opinions of other parties. Someone who has been offended can choose not to carry a grudge. A leadership team can adopt practices that lead to forgiveness and reconciliation, thus making the way for peace. Folk may choose to consciously and creatively

---

[7] Kenneth C. Haugk, Antagonists in the Church: How to Identify and Deal with Destructive Conflict (Minneapolis: Augsburg, 1988), 59.
[8] Hugh F. Halverstadt, Managing Church Conflict (Louisville: Westminster/John Knox, 1991). See also: John Kotter, Leading Change (Cambridge, MA: Harvard Business School Publishing, 1996); David B. Lott, ed., Conflict Management in Congregations (Bethesda, MD: The Alban Institute. 2001); Karl Slaikeu, Controlling the Costs of Conflict (San Francisco: Jossey-Bass, 1998); Peter Steinke, Healthy Congregations (Bethesda, MD: The Alban Institute, 1996); Ron Susek, Firestorm: Preventing and Overcoming Church Conflicts (Grand Rapids: Baker Books, 1999).

utilize concepts, doctrines and rituals, activities and projects that build a sense of community and serve as reminders of our need to be stewards of God's gifts. Finally, folk may simply come to accept the standard truth of all Church unity: the Church belongs to God.

THE ICHABOD EFFECT

The books of Samuel provide some valuable insights concerning the rise, fall, and subsequent reformation of the national economy of Israel—matters that are useful for congregations that are seeking to overcome dysfunctional mindsets and seasons of turnaround.
As part of the covenant economy, the congregation of Israel enjoyed the bountiful rewards of a fruitful and formidable witness with Yahweh whose providentially authoritative presence would be a light to the nations. The Ark of the Covenant would serve as a sign and symbol that the glory of God's presence rested with the congregation. However, as their prosperity soon slipped into sloth, the Hebrews turned from God by making wrong choices. Money became king. Eventually they came to the place where the presence of God was no longer among them.

During a decisive battle, the Ark of the Covenant was lost and with it Israel's confidence that God would defend and deliver them from all their enemies. The pregnant daughter-in-law of Eli, the head priest, lost both her husband and brother-in-law in the battle. When Eli himself died upon hearing the news of the Ark's capture, the daughter-in-law went into labor. She gave birth to a son, but she died during the delivery. The Bible states that the woman who was acting as the midwife named the son Ichabod. "Ichabod" means the glory has departed. "The glory has departed from Israel, for the ark of God has been captured" (1 Sam. 4:21).

The ethos of the urban Church resembles Ichabod. Depression breeds toxicity. Dysfunction creates fragmentation. Throughout this analytical narrative we have discussed how congregational dysfunction mars the public and communal role of the Church. Yet this weakened congregational witness cannot be separated from the stresses and illnesses that plague the broader community. The decline of the moral sector is both cause and consequence of the fragmentation and disorientation we see in the social, educational, and financial sectors.

With loss of jobs, breakup of families, and the dismantling of the school system, many urban dwellers have experienced drastic and traumatic changes. Social deprivation and cultural decline typically carry perilous psychological encumbrances as many congregations nostalgically scratch and claw to retain the rituals that once gave them hope. We who remain as spiritual leaders in these reforming contexts ignore the ominous signs of the pervasive identity crisis that afflicts us all.[9] Symptoms often function to disguise real troubles. For example, a decline in attendance may signal dissatisfaction with a decision, but it may also be a sign that many individuals have lost economic or social class status. Fewer families in the Church may indicate a need to broaden the ministry scope, but it may also point to the issue of the lack of marriageability of many poor urban men. Building decline may be a sign of decreased property value in a specific area, but it can also be a sign of the general malaise that sets in during a time of economic crisis.

The Church must face this sordid reality and change in order to survive. All urban Churches have to deal with major losses and drastic changes. Urban life can be difficult, but it can also be the source of meaningful relationships and advancements. How congregations address the coming reality will be critical to how they survive now and how they prepare for the future. Traditional

---

[9] Depression steals the joy of giving. Depressed people do not want give others the gifts of time, talent, and treasure, let alone the gift of the faith which is in Christ. Without giving, Christians cannot live; they become dead on the vine.

structures, rituals, and worship must be revised and refined to meet social, technological, and psychological realities.

BLESSED ARE THE POOR IN SPIRIT

> *"For the High and Exalted One who lives forever, whose name is Holy says this: 'I live in a high and holy place, and with the oppressed and lowly of spirit, to revive the spirit of the lowly and revive the heart of the oppressed'"* (Is. 57:15).

Depression saps congregational vigor and vision. More and more pastors report that when conflicts arise in the Church, they are often accompanied by higher stress levels, anxiety, and even physical illness. Without proper attention to the underlying systemic issues that affect urban communities, congregants are powerless to address not only the needs of the community but their own needs as well.

I have found Ed Stetzer's work on religion and mental illness for CNN to be instrumental for delineating the perceptions and predicaments around depression in American congregations:

• There are people in the pews every week—ministers, too—struggling with mental illness or depression.

• People of faith know that God has freed them to love others, and that love extends to everyone, even (and sometimes especially) those we don't understand.

• Christians need to affirm the value of medical treatment for mental illness.

• Compassion and care can go a long way in helping people know they don't have to hide.

- Mental illness has nothing to do with you or your family's beliefs. It can impact everyone.[10]

Reports show that prayer and fasting alone are not sufficient disciplines or resources for handling depression.[11] This is due in part to the fact that most people in the Church treat depression as the kind of illness or sin that can be cast out. It is interesting to note that many Christians will go to the doctor if they have cancer, a toothache, or a back problem, but they think prayer is sufficient enough to cure serious mental illness. While prayer and fasting are critical to the work of deliverance, we are still instructed to seek the best available help from professionals.

To address the issue of depression, both within the congregation and in the broader community, Church leaders must affirm these truths:

- The Church is a safe space for those who are battling depression and other mental illness.

- The Church sees its call to address mental illness as central to its tasks of deliverance, mission, evangelism, and discipleship.

- Christ's community of care and compassion is no respecter of persons. The Church reaffirms this ethic in regard to ethnic origin, economic condition, gender, age, and mental states and disabilities of its constituents.

---

[10] Ed Stetzer, "My Take on How Churches Can Respond to Mental Illness," CNN.com, April 7, 2013. http://religion.blogs.cnn.com/2013/04/07/my-take-how-Churches-can-respond-to-mental-illness/
[11] Ed Stetzer, "My Take on How Churches Can Respond to Mental Illness," CNN.com, April 7, 2013. http://religion.blogs.cnn.com/2013/04/07/my-take-how-Churches-can-respond-to-mental-illness/

- The goal to affirm the sacred dignity of all human beings is part of the Church's response to God's demand for love, mercy, and justice in the light of the Kingdom.

- As the body of Christ, the community of the faithful affirms the worth of all humanity and the value of interrelationship in all of God's creation.

- Those suffering depression and other mental illness are not deficient beings. They are conduits of God's grace. They can bring their gifts and resources to inform the shape of the ministry and further God's Kingdom on earth.

Below is a list of five goals that congregations can adopt regarding mental illness:

- Congregations must acknowledge depression as a very real presence in the lives of individual persons and families.

- The Church must accommodate and affirm in sensitive ways families and persons struggling with mental illness.

- The Church must view depression as a treatable rather than an incurable disease.

- The Church must develop a biblical and caring model for reaching out to someone with a mental illness. This includes clergy training in mental illness terminology and crisis intervention.

- The Church must acknowledge that it cannot address this challenge in isolation. Congregations should seek ways of building bridges with and working with mental health systems and providers, sources of information and support, and insurance and legal advisors.

CHAPTER SEVEN

KILLING ME SOFTLY:
THE GODS OF MAMMON

Gallantly, ceaselessly, quietly, man must fight for inner liberty to remain independent of the enslavement of the material world. Inner liberty depends upon being exempt from domination of things as well as from domination of people. There are many who have acquired a high degree of political and social liberty, but only very few are not enslaved to things. This is our constant problem—how to live with people and remain free, how to live with things and remain independent.
—Abraham Joshua Heschel, The Sabbath

I shop therefore I am.
—American Slogan

Every day advertisements tell us that we can find fulfillment and satisfaction in some sort of product – whether it's a television to provide entertainment, a car to provide adventure, a gadget to save time and money, or a sofa to give rest. Each of these products claims to have an answer to our need. And we believe them. After all, this is what we have been told will achieve for us the "perfect life." The problem is that we can spend our lives pursuing this dream only to discover that the products fail to

> deliver. In fact, in a twist of irony, these very items end up taking more of our enjoyment, adventure, time and money than they have given!
> —Augie Iadicicco, "Redeemer By the Sea"

> And be ye not conformed to this world, but b ye transformed by the renewing of your mind, that ye may prove what is good and acceptable, and perfect will of God.
> —Rom. 12:1

> For where your treasure is there will your heart be also.
> —Mt. 6:21

Our culture of Disney-style fantasy and gilded optimism serves as a thin veil covering the deep hollowness that pervades contemporary American life. We are routinely bombarded by images that drill into us one universal forceful message: money is king. The unrestrained desire for success and status drives the orgiastic epidemic of sensuality that invades our lives. Our love affair with gild and greed is feted on every level of the media. Our cinemas are filled with movies such as "The Great Gatsby," "The Wolf of Wall Street," "Confessions of a Shopaholic," and "The Devil Wears Prada." These movies celebrate the American religion of greed, passing off hyper-materialism as an epic quality to be handed down from one generation to the next. Yet in many urban communities, these images of excessive materialism frequently lead to the disintegration of traditional values, in part because American fantasy is taking place under a climate of rising expectations of economic prosperity. Materialism, of course, is the great impostor; it poses as a way to make us more than who we are. It claims to be an antidote to mental despair and self-questioning and markets itself as an expression of success.

THE AMERICAN INDIVIDUAL: CITIZEN OR CONSUMER?

Robert Putnam's powerful study of American civic fragmentation, Bowling Alone, provides a detailed account of how the American cult of individualism carries relevance decades later. According to Putnam, the private life of the individual has been enshrined and celebrated at the expense of substantive civic and public engagements. Individuals no longer find investment in civic organizations pleasurable or desirable. The web of community organization and civic associations that once supplied Americans a viable space to work out their vocational identities, invest their talents, and deepen their ethical horizons has become largely obsolete. Person-to-person interactions that were once crucial to the social fabric of American life have frayed. In the wake of these realities, trust, cooperation, and information sharing are declining moral commodities. The social loss of this shift is immeasurable: increased isolation, stress, anger, divorce, homelessness, crime—the list goes on.

The cult of private lifestyles in large measure feeds public confusion. A culture of desire and consumption tends to withhold investment in civic formations. Indeed, cars, the Internet, tablets, digital chat rooms, pornography, and mass entertainment that flood urban America serve as an index for civic disengagement and social indifference. The fact that we spend more and more time engaged in private and insulated consumption is a sign of severe social fragmentation. Urban America is very much part and parcel of the national culture of frenzied spending and status seeking.

Without productive citizen participation, the revival of public life in the city is a Sisyphean affair. The variegated life of the city may permit more social interaction but not necessarily more social cooperation. Cities have become sprawling theatres of contiguous yet anonymous interaction: ethnic, media, technological, ideological, and financial "scapes."[1] However, these are of little substance when it comes to building faculties of trust, cooperation, and broad scale multicultural, multiethnic, and multidenominational alliances. Community organizations such as the NAACP, The National Urban League, the Boys Club, SNCC, and Core, as well as Churches, denominations, synods, and synagogues, are at the top of this list. Along with the decline of participation in public life and the loss of the elements of social capital—care, concern, information sharing, etc.—is the decline and disrepair of social amenities.

The lack of quality social amenities has also fueled the vast psychic exodus from urban life. With fewer resources being poured into schools, parks, and community centers, there is a widening feeling of isolation and indifference, regardless of class or culture. When police are seen as military operatives (read public enemies), when politicians are viewed as narrow and narcissistic charlatans, when unions are seen as tribal gangs, when public schools are compared to sewers of mediocrity, and when religious establishments are considered citadels of xenophobic intolerance or moral triumphalism, then civic esteem and social honor diminishes. Private indulgence increases. Persons simply turn inwards or to their tribe, clan, or tradition, no matter how anti-democratic or socially regressive these enclaves are. The result is deeper social anonymity, greater civic polarization, cultural degradation, and the flight from authority. The primary agenda driving contemporary citizenship patterns is, "What's in it for me?" The University of Wisconsin-Madison has produced a far-reaching study on the complex relationship between capital accumulation, the rise in personal spending, and social capital. The study concludes that the

---

1 Here I rely on the work of Arjun Appadurai and Elijah Anderson. Arjun Appadurai, "Disjuncture and Difference in the Global Cultural Economy" from Modernity at Large: Cultural Dimensions of Globalization, (Minneapolis: University of Minnesota Press, 1996), 27-47; Elijah Anderson, Code of the Street: Decency, Violence, and the Moral Life of the Inner City (New York: W.W. Norton, 1999),150-154; Elijah Anderson, Streetwise: Race, Class and Change in an Urban Community (Chicago: University of Chicago Press, 1990).

burden of overconsumption has had a deleterious effect on social safety. Here are some of the study's more interesting findings:

- The deterioration of public schools has led to increased enrollment in private schools.

- The deterioration of policing and public safety has led to the rise of gated communities.

- The deterioration of public recreation facilities has led to private swimming clubs and private home pools. People tend to just stay home.
- The deterioration of public transportation has led to more reliance on individually owned vehicles. [2]

It says further:

> In each of these cases, the deterioration of public goods generates a vicious cycle: as the more affluent pull out of public goods consumption they reduce their political support for the provision of those public goods which–since they are politically influential–leads to a further deterioration of the public goods, which leads to more people withdrawing to private, more costly, substitutes. This cycle fuels consumerism–the intensified preoccupation with private consumption. [3]

Churches are both villain and victim in this process. Churches build social capital by providing a safe place for people to work on common interests, share ideals, and build relationships. Yet congregations that used to be forums of civic engagement are losing ties to urban constituents. The current trend in worship is to get people in and out of a pre-packaged worship mode. Many who attend worship

---
[2] Eric Olin Wright and Joel Rogers, American Society: How It Really Works (NY: W. W. Norton, 2010). See also http://www.ssc.wisc.edu/~wright/ContemporaryAmericanSociety/Chapter%207%20—%20consumerism%20—%20Norton%20August.pdf.
[3] Ibid.

on Sunday do not interact with Church leadership or others in the pews throughout the week. Many worshippers acknowledge that they attend large Churches in order to avoid much accountability or responsibility, though this is certainly not true of all who attend or serve large Churches. They may simply choose not to add another round of commitments to their overworked and overspent lives. They may indulge in a religion of consumerism that helps them actualize their dreams without having to contribute to a broader congregational or community life. They may be attracted to the preaching, singing, or even the large, impressive Church building. They may come to get a quick fix but perhaps not be authentically transformed or truly healed.

Our culture of consumption, what the perceptive Daniel Bell once called the "institutionalization of envy,"[4] is largely driven by the media with its endless assault of advertising. The related culture of individualism makes us vulnerable to the media onslaught, causing more and more individuals to go into debt and develop deeper anxiety and mental isolation. According to Juliet Schor, advertisers are the main culprits. She writes:

> *When twenty-somethings can't afford much more than a utilitarian studio but think they should have a New York apartment to match the ones they see on "Friends," they are setting unattainable consumption goals for themselves, with dissatisfaction as a predictable result. When the children of affluent suburban and impoverished inner-city households both want the same Tommy Hilfiger logo emblazoned on their chests and the top-of-the-line Swoosh on their feet, it's a potential disaster. One solution to these problems emerged on the talk-show circuit recently, championed by a pair of young urban "entry-level" earners: live the faux life, consuming as if you had a big bank balance. Their strategies? Use your expense account for private entertainment, date bankers, and sneak into snazzy parties without an invitation.*

---

4 Daniel Bell, The Cultural Contradictions of Capitalism, (New York: Basic Books, 1976), 15-25.

Haven't got the wardrobe for it? No matter. Charge expensive clothes, wear them with the tags on, and return them the morning after. Apparently the upscale life is now so worth living that deception, cheating, and theft are a small price to pay for it. These are the more dramatic examples. Millions of us face less stark but problematic comparisons every day. People in one-earner families find themselves trying to live the lifestyle of their two-paycheck friends. Parents of modest means struggle to pay for the private schooling that others in their reference group have established as the right thing to do for their children. [5]

CHOICE, CHILDREN, AND CONSUMPTION

Children have become a prime target for companies seeking to capitalize on American and global spending trends. Infants are being increasingly targeted by advertisers. Images that bombard children are luring them into a buying practice that many adults have not comprehended, let alone resisted. Little wonder, then, that a child with no savings account can find the money to pay for the newest Nintendo or Xbox, and families can find ways to get to Disneyworld but will not find the means for their children to go on mission trips, to pay for additional academic resources, or to engage in programs that promote spiritual growth and moral formation. Many children often value themselves and their peers in light of the ability to own certain things or enjoy certain experiences. So poor urban children sucked in by the market machine develop low self-esteem because they have little access to those things and experiences that lend status. According to Trent Hamm and Juliet Schor:

> *Children today are more likely to have emotional and mental disorders and are much more likely to be out of shape and*

---

[5] Juliet B. Shor, The Overspent American: Upscaling: Downshifting, and the New Consumer (New York: HarperPerennial, 1998), 5. For another perspective on the invasive and exploitative power of spending, see David Carter, "How Advertising Manipulates Your Choices and Spending Habits (and What to Do About It)," http://lifehacker.com/5824328/how-advertising-manipulates-your-choices-and-spending-habits-and-what-to-do-about-it.

> overweight. The psychology of materialism and materialist values has negative effects on an adult mind, but on the mind of a child who has not yet learned many of the things adults take for granted, the effects of materialism can be tremendous – and feelings of insufficiency that are pervasive in modern marketing lead children to a negative self-image (that, of course, can only be pacified through more consumer goods). [6]

The real danger of materialism is that it takes on excessive religious fervor and promises great rewards to its adherents, rewards that are unattainable. Both Plato and Paul remind modern Americans that being enslaved to wealth robs us of the most noble riches and highest virtues of life. The challenge for the American poor is that success is too often crudely collapsed into status. It is assumed that one's character is defined by one's currency and that wellbeing is closely tied to wealth. The urban ethos then is saturated with fake emblems of a dream in which the pursuit of material excess and visible prosperity is greater than life itself. The "gangsterization" subtly forced into acceptability through subliminal advertisements of America is no worse than our need to exploit others for the sake of financial rewards. One does not have to look far into the recesses of American history to find where this brutality comes from.

One must continually feed these gods of wealth and status in such a way that one's loyalties and energies are driven towards the attainment of status, style, power, and prestige. The cribs, clothes, and cars become a way for us to be both visible and desirable in this culture. What is lost is the cultivation of the moral and intellectual virtues that are needed to make life meaningful. Respect for persons, appreciation for the arts and nature, and the

regard for tradition all lose currency in the current context of moral revisionism. In our hunt for status and self-fulfillment we become

---

[6] Trent Hamm, "Review: Born to Buy - The Simple Dollar," Nov 2, 2007. Book review of Juliet B. Shor, Born to Buy: the Commercialized Child and the New Consumer Culture (NY: Scribner, 2005). http://www.thesimpledollar.com/review-born-to-buy/

self-centered and cut off from community. The "American dream" has become the shabbiest form of social one-upmanship, defined by luxury goods, lavish styles, and less accountability. Herman Edwards, former NFL star and sports analyst, said, "Many troubles are avoided when you live a simple life."[7] People need the ability to distinguish between wants and needs. Many Americans suffer from an "embarrassment of riches." According to Pulitzer Prize winning journalist Ellen Goodman:

> *Normal is getting dressed in clothes that you buy for work and driving through traffic in a car that you are still paying for, in order to get to the job you need to pay for the clothes and the car, and the house you leave vacant all day so you can afford to live in it.*[8]

Indeed, our search for more has left us drowning in the wasteland of unfulfilled potential. We have given up our souls for much ado about nothing. Our naked avarice has led to a certain affirmation of phoniness. Materialism seduces the self. When this happens, a person is incapable of the surrender ethic needed to invest in positive relationships that focus on the good of others. What follows are a deflation of one's true self-worth and a shattering of one's moral energies. We become passive and find ourselves devoid of initiative and zeal. The lie of materialism surfaces when we realize that we cannot be truly led or fed or bought or taught by our fantasies. Indeed, while many Americans hunger for wealth and status, the majority of Americans have been locked out of these "fruits of prosperity." Countless people, many of them in urban areas, are left to scratch and scramble for the crumbs that fall from the table. Christians are called to offer the truth of where our treasure lies while caring for those who suffer from the various consequences of poverty.

---

[7] Herman Edwards, "Sportscenter" on ESPN, May 29, 2014.
[8] Quotation from Ellen Goodman, as found in Megan Pacheo, "Has Debt Become our Therapy?" Crosswalk, February 26, 2014. www.crosswalk.com/.../has-debt-become-ourtherapy.htm..

Spiritual discipline can provide a "handle on reality." In order for us to be compassionate, we must be torn from the deceptive mother of our base desires. Of course, we have to battle against fears, phobias, and ignorance. Too often we confuse small wants and desires with God's will. We must have our Damascus road experience in order to be compassionate and to know that God's will is much larger than our wants and our desires. Our purpose is to fulfill God's purpose for our lives. Compassion involves a shattering and a fragmentation. The base idol that governs our thinking must be broken in order for us to have a sense of civitas, a willingness to sacrifice our individual agendas for the health of our collective wellbeing. Without this prerequisite we remain situated within our strongholds—unmoved, bound, and frozen. The Holy Spirit breaks in with good news and concretizes the shattering of the old to prepare the fecund soil of a new urban Jerusalem. Embodied in the words of the Lausanne Congress is the spirit of social reform, "The evangel is God's Good News in Jesus Christ. . . . It is Good News of liberation, of restoration, of wholeness, and of salvation that is personal, social, global and cosmic."[9]

CONSUMERISM AND SELF-DECEPTION

Earlier we attempted to demonstrate that discipleship is spiritual warfare—a ceaseless taxing and policing of the ego, a struggle against the nagging, relentless desires of flesh. In regards to our collective wellbeing, consumerism may well be the most prohibitive bulwark against the wholesale work of the Spirit in our lives. Without overcoming the personal demons of self-deception and self-righteousness, one is weak against the perfidy of this social maelstrom. Consumerism's shameless championing of excess is lethal because its subtle poisons infect the civil fabric of credibility

---

9 Ronald J. Sider, Good News and God Works: A Theology for the Whole Gospel (Grand Rapids: Baker Books, 1993), 79.

and legitimacy. American preaching and politics have been known to serve as willing handmaidens in this drama, cloaking self-aggrandizement and narrow private consumption. The cult of possibility thinking and self-help can quickly lead to an attempt to misuse God and the Bible for the glorification of material happiness and greed. Avarice is airbrushed and reworked to fit what is best for everyone else. We deceive ourselves by leaving unexamined the true intentions behind our speech, actions, and desires. Haunted by the disease of more, we overlook the needs and concerns of others.

An inflated sense of importance leads to a distorted perspective of life, and one's estimation of what is essential to live a life of dignity and possibility becomes obscured, jaded, and misplaced. For example, we can be obsessed with a hobby, a pastime, a trade, a talent, a gift, or another person. When we devote enough energy to something outside of God's will, we lose our moral anchoring and slide into idol worship that undermines the integration of the soul and a balanced lifestyle. A fine demonstration of self-deception and self-obsession is seen in the parable of the Pharisee and the tax collector in Luke 18:9-14:

> *Two men went up to the temple to pray, one a Pharisee, the other a tax collector. The Pharisee stood and prayed thus with himself, "God, I thank you that I am not like other men, extortioners, unjust, adulterers or even as this tax collector."*

This parable illustrates the spiritual and moral confusion that takes place when a person's identity is wrapped up with the hunger for image and status: the question of how I look to others takes priority over whether my life is pleasing to God. Our relationship with God is characterized by the battle between our capacity to focus on God's will for our lives and our tendency to be distracted by lesser gods. Faith is the ability to focus on the will of God amidst worldly distractions and demonic obstructions. The story reveals that God is not concerned with the obvious visual entrapments of human righteous, nor does He focus on our roles and responsibilities within the political, social, or religious structures that shape human affairs. Rather, what the parable highlights is that God is most attuned to what constitutes our values and what occupies us inwardly. What gives us meaning? What issues govern our souls? Do we really seek to be obedient to his commands? His word? His will, His way? Do we hunger for His presence? Do we understand the true power of His grace? Are we concerned about knowing Him?

The Pharisee deceived himself. He presumed his ritualistic practices guarded him from the matters of the heart, so he was blind to the ultimate relationship that gave fasting and tithing currency. To think that his occupation had kept him from sinning was a sign of his level of self-deception. To hide behind religious ritual or the form of righteousness is to fall into the most powerful traps of Satan. In fact, the Bible paints the Pharisee as a tragic figure; he simply missed the point. His ritual activities or his valuation of them prevented him from getting to the real, rough, and raw issues of life. We must understand that human capacity, ritual, or prayers are no matches for the wiles of Satan outside of the Holy Spirit.

Too many believers live out similar sentiments. The Pharisee, like many of us, expressed thankfulness for his moral achievements and material well-being. We are to give thanks for health, strength, relationships, resources, wisdom, talents, the body of Christian salvation, and much more. The problem with the Pharisee was the way in which he minimized his own faults, failures, and foibles through wrongly comparing himself with a person in another station of life. He was self-obsessed, yet unable to examine his own soul. While the Pharisee chose to operate in isolation from God, we are all called to invite the Holy Spirit to join with us, to make us aware of our hearts and the hearts of others. We experience the work of the Holy Spirit as comforter and co-sufferer. In ministering to the brokenhearted, God's children are delivered as the Holy Comforter works with us, enabling us to cope with and overcome great odds through daily struggles and contradictions. God on the cross helps us to bear our own crosses because we have freely chosen to bear the cross of Christ. In this way human beings become more Christ-like because they have elected to move into His suffering as He is wounded on behalf of the suffering. This Holy Spirit counsels us and comforts us in order to lead us to address our own sin, allowing us to be more compassionate of others.

Consumerism is a mask. Shielding our flight from pride and prejudice, it hides our true being behind polish and pomp, secluded from the judging, scrutinizing gaze of an invasive world. Through the manufacturing of a fantastic, airbrushed existence, we are able to live in the gilded moment of an extended future, a state that is never fully realized, leaving us emptier than before. Civic myopia is the wayward child of such spiritual licentiousness. We lack the requisite ingredients to build moral bonds of community and solidarity. A culture of dysfunction is born. Material possessions become outlets for soul hunger. Relationships become malls for those addicted to hollow highs. No wonder, in a society obsessed with status and privilege, style and prestige, friendships are things to be exploited and leveraged for personal gain. Persons are trophies. Associates are political statements. Connection is currency. Marriage is a commodity that forfeits its original value, and friendship is less about mutual sharing and authentic empowering than it is about personal networking. The worth of any relational bond is measured with the index of what you can do for me. When such happens, values such as real intimacy, sacrifice, appreciation, solidarity, justice, equality, fellowship, and fairness of nature quickly fade in the sand.

It's not that material entities count for nothing. Certainly clothing, shelter, and food are essential to the health of the body and wellbeing of families and communities. The disease of consumerism is that the addiction to more is making us less human, less authentic, and less moral. Richard John Neuhaus clarifies consumerism as "living in a manner that is measured by having rather than being."[10] The need to acquire has come to dominate our lives to the exclusion of just about every other value. Jesus did not say, "Man shall not live by bread"; He said that bread alone will not help us to live a life of character. Read carefully:

> *Be careful that you do not forget the Lord your God, failing to observe his commands, his laws and his decrees that I am giving you this day. Otherwise, when you eat and are satisfied, when you build fine houses and settle down, and when your herds and flocks grow large and your silver and gold increase and all you have is multiplied, then your heart will become proud and you will forget the Lord your God, who brought you out of Egypt, out of the land of slavery. (Deut. 8:11-14)*

In response to our present social dread, the Church must combine an ethic of modesty and simplicity in light of the discipline of redemptive suffering. Paul tells Timothy to "endure hardship" (2 Tim. 2:3). The enormous energy spent masking our self-loathing has only intensified our predicament, increasing our tolerance to the awful disease of soul murder and foreclosing on constructive adventures to develop realizable moral visions for a more just and peaceable future. From a Pauline perspective, the denial of suffering prevents us from understanding and appreciating the depth of our fallibility and fallenness. Vulnerability opens the critical space of personal and communal deliverance. Woundedness occasions true worship. Within such a curriculum we learn the true grammar of the cross: not to flee from the wild, absurd exigencies of this life but

---

[10] Richard John Neuhaus, Doing Well and Doing Good (NY: Doubleday, 2012), 51.

to face life's wretched riddles as co-workers of Christ, armed with prayer and hope, courageously confronting the dragon of narcissism as we speak prophetic truth to various status quos in love—come what may! Such is holy witness. It is the discipline of working with and struggling against our selfish, prideful, ego-driven tendencies that teaches us to become fully human and mature Christians. In short, compassion can only be learned within community, within the deep, dramatic flows of complex and fragile relationships. At its core, the human situation is part tragic and part comic. In those proclivities that are expressed when friends get sick, when children are obstinate, when spouses exercise unusual behavior, when loved ones reach their limit, or when an emergency comes up, we learn the awesome yet strange ways of God.

The Church can help combat the specter of narcissism in the following ways by preaching a Gospel of total well-being, of balance, and of interconnectedness.

- Encourage contentment and simplicity as spiritual disciplines.

- Promote daily physical exercise as a form of spiritual growth.

- Promote an ethic of character development over consumption.

- Encourage less television watching and more reading, meditation, and the power of exploration.

- Reform and recast artistic forums to celebrate non-market values and virtues.

- Celebrate sacrificial giving regardless of social location or present financial condition.

- Teach Holy Communion as self-giving love and not merely an act of remembrance.

- Have special High Holy days of simplicity and sacrifice.

- Demonstrate how reckless consumerism in relationships threatens healthy intimacy and authenticity.

- Encourage Sabbath observation so that people find the rest in God and in matters of the Spirit that the rush to acquire and accomplish holds in check.

- Encourage people to purchase what they need, not simply what they want.

- In teaching about money matters, build on a biblical foundation and affirm the importance of the family.

- Adopt a Blessed Friday ethic. Rather than going out on Friday night to fuel the craze of consumerism, many Churches have designated the end of the workweek as "Blessed Friday." These Churches have lifted up blessing others over buying and shopping.

- Teach youth about finances and stewardship. Biblical stewardship is not simply about paying tithes and offerings, but about reconstituting how and why we live—a revaluation of lifestyle. Stewardship permits positive preparation for the future, the rising costs of education and healthcare, the costs of maintaining a Church.

- And perhaps above all, move the Church from the popular and "traditional" Church models toward "missional" structures that release believers to serve in meaningful ways that make a difference for themselves and others.

Compassion, like charity, begins at home, in the home of the heart. We believers must find a way to practice compassion as an antidote to the rabid individualism that infects our common life together. The traditional values of self-worth (the positive appreciation of one's soul and service) and self-discipline (the psychic labor required for authentic personal betterment) must be recovered and refined for the sake of spiritual and communal housecleaning. The "homesomeness" of compassion invites constant rehabilitation, seasoning, and sharpening. It must be revisited over and over again to meet the growing demands of an ever-changing existence. For compassion to take root, it must meet the stresses of life where they are. It must stretch where relationships stretch. God, being our model, says, "I will never leave thee nor forsake thee" (Deut. 31:6) and "Lo, I am with you always, even unto the end of the world" (Mt. 28:20). We are bound to endure the pain of others. It is in the measured, patient endurance, the longsuffering, that the journey to wholeness is made.

CHAPTER EIGHT

GOD BLESS THE CHILD THAT'S GOT HIS OWN:

RISING DEBT AND INCOME INEQUALITY

The greatest country, the richest country, is not that which has the most capitalists, monopolists, immense grabbings, vast fortunes, with its sad, sad soil of extreme, degrading, damning poverty, but the land in which there are the most homesteads, freeholds—where wealth does not show such contrasts high and low, where all men have enough—a modest living—and no man is made possessor beyond the sane and beautiful necessities.
       —Walt Whitman

RICH AND POOR

An ever-widening gap exists between the rich and poor and between the west and other lands around the world. Our pursuit of riches and possessions, our fondness for gadgets and technology, and our quest for luxury and leisure in modern capitalist economies has hardened us against the plight of the poor and marginal citizens of the world. In fact, we have found sophisticated ways both to justify our harshness and to numb our senses against the savage living of so many in our cities. Ron Sider has written:

> *Rich Christians must be careful not to distort the biblical teaching that God sometimes rewards obedience with material abundance. Wealthy persons who make Christmas baskets and give them to relief agencies have not satisfied God's demands. God wills justice for the poor, not occasional charity. And justice means things like the jubilee and the sabbatical remission of debts. It means economic structures that guarantee all people access to the productive resources needed to earn a decent living. Prosperity without a kind of biblical concern for justice unambiguously signifies disobedience.* [1]

North America has become a "land of desire,"[2] to use the apt title of William Leach's provocative book. There is no apology for the ostentatious and voracious pursuit of wealth. It is a celebration of greed and a glorification of the virtues of entrepreneurialism and free market capitalism. The political system has served to protect and defend these financial interests because more and more policies were constructed to ensure that more wealth was concentrated in fewer hands. America's gargantuan pursuit of wealth created less compassion for those who did not enjoy wealth or who had little part in American economic success.

During the 1980's there was an enormous increase in income for those who were already wealthy, giving rise to the adage that the rich got richer. This took place when working-class Americans experienced stagnation in their income levels and a significant segment of the population existed well under the poverty line. For the majority of Americans, incomes did not keep up with the rise in prices for goods and services or inflation rates. The net result of

---
1 Ronald Sider, Rich Christians in an Age of Hunger (Nashville: Thomas Nelson, 2005), 103.
2 William Leach, Land of Desire: Merchants, Power, and the Rise of a New American Culture (New York: Random House, 1993)

this combination of public policy, wealth accumulation, and free market interests was the intensification of inequality, decreased economic mobility, and the hardening and thickening of the walls between rich and poor.

RISING DEBT

These rapid changes in the economy bring to our families unprecedented levels of uncertainty and anxiety. The war in Iraq has cost billions of dollars and incalculable loss in terms of moral and social equity. Indeed, it has generated increasing distrust not simply of public offices and politicians themselves, but of the very meaning of America itself. It may take several generations to restore the damage done to our collective psyche. The housing and loan scandal has retarded an already scrambled economy, adding to the quiet desperation of America's middle and working classes. Higher education seems to have become a cash cow for the university as big business. Many of those who are shut out of the economy, i.e. those who make up the underclass, have become vagabonds, re-introduced to homelessness, crime, or despair. These people are left to fend for themselves in a world spiraling out of control. The steady relocation of jobs overseas threatens a fragile social base. The immigration issue continues to expose our inability to come to terms with ourselves as a nation along the lines of race, history, and economics. Needless to say, during hard times most human beings without a sufficient moral compass surrender to fear and futility, resorting to the most uncivil parts of their social pasts.

A recent study, "The Challenge of Credit Card Debt for the African American Middle Class,"[3] coauthored by Demos and the NAACP, details the connection between debt and income inequality in our society. The strain of harsh economic conditions often forces

---

3 See more: http://www.naacp.org/pages/the-challenge-of-credit-card-debt-for-the-african-american-middle-class.

many poor and working-class American families to rely heavily on credit cards to handle basic household responsibilities. African Americans, for example, are more likely to pay higher interest rates on credit cards and on auto loans as well as suffer more from the negative consequences of debt than other ethnic groups. More than three million Americans could fall below the federal poverty line and several million others just above it because of overwhelming interest rates they pay on their credit card bills each month.

According to Robert Scott, the poverty level for a family of four with two children is $21,834. Debt-poor households of four carried an average of $25,600 in obligations with annual interest payments of $2,250 per year.[4] When one compares this to the numbers from the Bureau of Labor Statistics showing that the bottom fifth of American households reported an average income of a less than $10,000, then the math becomes quickly evident: these households are spending more than twice as much as they are taking in. "This makes sense, because when people have bad years, they draw down their savings, or they borrow to try and stabilize their living standard,"[5] says Nicholas Eberstadt, an economist at AEI. Updating how the government measures poverty, let alone the tall task of re-energizing the economy, is an uphill battle, laden with political barriers. Pressman and Scott say: "If the poverty line is moved up, more people would become eligible for federal benefits, and with Congress in the mood to cut, it seems unlikely that updating the poverty measure would gain any political traction."[6]

"Use of credit in long term investments for the future is a specific African American problem, largely because of the historical

---

[4] Steve Pressman and Robert H. Scott III, "Consumer Debt and Poverty Measurement," Focus 27, 1 (Summer 2010).
[5] Jenna Zwang, "How Debt is Swelling the Ranks in American Poverty," National Journal (September 24, 2011) http://www.nationaljournal.com/economy/how-debt-is-swelling-ranks-of-americans-in-poverty-20110924
[6] Ibid.

impact of racism in wealth building, and current racial bias in lending," said study co-author and Demos policy analyst Catherine Ruethschlin.[7] In this study, researchers found that the seeds for economic disparities seen today were sown over 50 years of predatory lending.

According to the report, 80 percent of Black college grads took out some amount of loans for their education, compared to 65 percent of whites. Credit debt as a result of student loans can then affect career outcomes, as credit checks are sometimes part of the hiring process. Those with poor credit are often relegated to low-paying jobs due to this dubious but legal practice. In the study, an overwhelming 99 percent of indebted moderate-income African American households who had expenses related to starting or running a business in the past three years still carry that expense on their credit card bill.

UNEMPLOYMENT

The rate of joblessness, especially among African American men living in urban centers, is astonishing. This national problem is exacerbated greatly when we consider that the rise of urban America's unemployed parents has stemmed from a combination of factors: the collapse of manufacturing industries, a withdrawing of quality social amenities, and a lack of an imaginative civic-religious-economic network. Joblessness creates a diminishing prospect for marriage, and it tends to work against the stabilizing of the nuclear family. Though many ethnic minorities have developed kinship systems to mitigate the impact of unemployment, joblessness still threatens one's attitude towards his or her own success and self-worth. Not having a job leads to self-doubt which leads to anger with both oneself and others.

---

7 Jazelle Hunt, "Massive Credit Card Debt Threatens the African American Middle Class," Inland Valley News (January 2, 2014) http://inlandvalleynews.com/news/2014/jan/02/massive-credit-card-debt-threatens-african-america/

The rise in unemployment and the stagnation of wages leave too many people needing basic necessities. The people of the Church where I pastor are seeking to address some of those issues and are finding that the community is being transformed in more ways than one. In addition to providing coats, school supplies, food, and other resources for our neighbors, we also find that our neighbors want to join in to help provide these needs. While our current culture is rife with materialism and the desire for wealth, there is also a turn towards philanthropy and being aware of the needs of our neighbors. When the Church can show that this is true to the living out of the Kingdom of God, then the Spirit can work in the lives of people who both have needs that must be met and those who can help to meet the needs.

There are a variety of ways that congregations can help to address economic crises with their congregants. A climate of anxiety contributes to the slowdown in financial contributions, especially by Christians in mainline and evangelical congregations. One way to address financial worries is to try to create a culture of simplicity within the Church and encourage congregants to adopt similar practices at home. I discussed this more fully in Chapter 7. Another way is for the Church to launch into the deep waters of financial exploration. Urban residents need decent paying jobs. I want to offer some models for how congregations can engage in economic development with an eye toward building and sustaining credible social capital.

PERSONAL FINANCE AND BUDGETING: THE CONGREGATION AS PACESETTER

Congregations must seek God's voice in all matters. In a time of financial gerrymandering, spiritual leaders must place a premium on the serious study of scripture and pray for spiritual guidance on the subject of money management, especially on the issue of borrowing and debt.[8] It goes without saying that Christians can curb their spending habits. They can undergo stewardship challenges that prioritize saving. Here, I will enumerate some practices that can help eliminate excessive borrowing and debt by members.

First, recognize that God is the source of everything we have. As Lord of the cosmos, God has provided instructions for how we are to conduct our personal and family financial matters. Money undoubtedly influences our beliefs and behavior. Scriptures teach that the human heart follows our true treasures. Second Corinthians 9:10 says that God "who supplies seed for the sower and bread for food will also supply and increase your store of seed and will enlarge the harvest of your righteous." Matthew 6:26 reassures us that if God takes care of the birds, we can believe He is going to provide for us, too.

Second, believers must be encouraged to form relationships and networks with others in their peer groups who adopt simple lifestyles. Frugality is the recipe for financial freedom, a genuine witness to a world that longs for shelter from the storm of economic uncertainty and deliverance from a culture of mammon. Luke 19:17 tells us that God is pleased when we are faithful and trustworthy in minor things.

Third, develop a schedule to pay off outstanding debts. By prioritizing our debts we can tackle them more efficiently. What debts have the highest interest rates? How many payments are left? Focus efforts on paying off one debt ahead of schedule, and then continue on to the next one.

---

[8] Please consult Floyd H. Flake, The African-American Church Management Book (Valley Forge: Judson Press, 2005).

Fourth, save for a better future. The average American saves two percent of his or her monthly income. One recommended structure is the "10-10-80 rule":

- Tithe: 10 percent
- Save: 10 percent
- Use for living: 80 percent

And finally, the use of credit cards should be allowed for convenience as long as you pay them off at the end of the month. While it is difficult to avoid borrowing for education and to purchase a home, credit card usage can be controlled. That's why it's important to budget fastidiously. As authors Thomas Stanley and William Danko explain, "Planning and controlling consumption are key factors underlying wealth accumulation. . . . Operating a household without a budget is akin to operating a business without a plan, without goals, and without direction."[9] Keep account of your spending. Good budgeting involves not just the structuring and allocation of money and resources, but tracking receipts and credit card uses. The implementation of a credible spending plan may be tedious at first, but it promises to yield dividends in the future. For Mary Hunt, a seasoned personal finance consultant and advisor to many Christians, "It's the discretionary expenses that often get consumers into financial trouble. These include entertainment, recreation, vacations, discretionary clothing, and other incidentals. When you cut these expenses, there is more money left to pay down debt and to save." Hunt says further, "Intelligent borrowing has a fair way to get out of the agreement, is secured with collateral, is for something that has a life expectancy of more than three years and will increase in value (so you won't be paying for a purchase long

---

[9] Stanley, Thomas, and William Danko. The Millionaire Next Door (New York: Pocket Books, 1996), 78; "The Millionaire Next Door." New York Times. 1997. 29 Nov 2007. http://www.nytimes.com/books/first/s/stanley-millionaire.html.

after it's no longer useful to you, or paying more for something than it's worth), and has a reasonable interest rate for the loan. [10]

Spiritual leaders can model healthy spending practices by how they develop and implement the Church's budget. A percentage of the budget can be set aside for community development. Congregations serve as living models of sound financial management and economic fluency. Below, I will explore some models for how congregations can help generate various forms of capital for their communities.

THE COMMUNITY-MINDED CHRISTIAN: SOCIAL TRUST THROUGH EMPLOYMENT AND EDUCATION

Urban communities that are able to establish the ligaments of social cooperation can build the foundation for jobs. Congregations working as partners have developed innovative strategies to channel economic opportunities in ways that help to address the paucity of social capital in many cities and towns.[11] Organizations like Thriving and Rebuild are focused on training Christian leaders who will help rebuild their urban communities.[12] I believe that Churches of any size can forge critical partnerships with other organizations in order to generate social capital. Through employment programs and educational opportunities, jobs can be created and other financial resources brought into the community.

As far back as 1977, Gil B. Lloyd wrote an article, "The Black Church and Economic Development,"[13] in which he portrayed the

---

10 Quoted in "Finances," http://www.crosswalk.com/family/finances/. See also Mary Hunt's book, Debt-Proof Living: How to Get out of Debt and Stay That Way (Grand Rapids: Revell, 2014).
11 For a few stellar examples please see Michael A. Battle, The African American Church at Work (St. Louis, MO: Hodale Press, 1994).
12 "Movements in Urban Church Planting and Leadership Development." http://thegospel-coalition.org/blogs/thabitianyabwile/2012/08/30/movements-in-urban-Church-planting-and-leadership-development/
13 Gil B. Lloyd, "The Black Church and Economic Development." Western Journal of Black Studies 1:4, Dec. 1977, 270-275.

congregation as a theater of economic fluency. Through tithes, offerings, and fundraising activities, Churches have been able to wield a degree of economic influence. Further, he argues that the Black Church, often in partnership with the federal government, has provided both a moral and economic impetus for the economic redevelopment of urban areas.

Ray Rivera, head of the Latino Pastoral Action Center in New York City, affirms a social ethic called "holistic evangelism"— a brand of Christianity that views spiritual growth as crucial to improving our material wellbeing and social circumstances. "Evangelism has to be holistic," says Rivera. "It is still not on the top of the list of priorities for the Church. But it's making the list now." Rivera's vision is that "holistic ministry will be the dominant paradigm of the Latino Church in the 21st century."[14] Urban clergy must continue to expand their capacity to institutionalize the gospel of social development. By building social capital with schools, banks, and other institutions, congregations can minister to the whole person. Working to provide educational and employment opportunities is one way in which the social gospel is being recast in 21st century.

In 2002, Amy Sherman, director of the Hudson Institute's Faith in Communities (FIC) initiative, collaborated with Dr. Jesse Miranda on a study of the outreach practices of Hispanic congregations.[15] The Hudson report revealed that Hispanic congregations and Church ministries have been vital to the generation of moral, social, and intellectual capital. Programs offered include food trusts, counseling services, economic development initiatives,

---

14 As quoted in Amy Sherman, "Good News from the Hispanic Church." http://www.centeronfic.org/v2/equip/publications/articles/good_news_Churches2.htm.
15 Amy L. Sherman, "The Community Serving Activities of Hispanic Protestant Congregations," popularly called the Hudson Report. http://www.webmail.centeronfic.org/articles/HispanicSurveyReport.pdf. Also produced from this study is "The National Resource Directory of Hispanic Compassion Ministries" (co-published, Hudson FIC and AMEN, 2003). Modeled on the membership directory of the Christian Community Development Association (CCDA), this directory includes a state-by-state listing of Hispanic congregations with operational community outreach programs.

afterschool programs, and educational institutions. Furthermore, a substantial number of Hispanic Churches are working with police departments, public schools, secular nonprofits, and county offices to improve the quality of life and alleviate poverty and social depression in their communities. For example, youth pastor Max Torres of El Tabernaculo Assembly of God in Houston, has worked with local public schools for the past twenty years to improve the test scores of Hispanic youth. [16]

Rev. Charles Adams, pastor of Hartford Memorial Baptist Church in Detroit, Michigan, provided some insight into how congregations implement the emerging gospel of economic development.

> *"The Church needs to concentrate on the business of creating economic institutions," declared Adams. "The issue is jobs. People being laid off through all this corporate downsizing is affecting every Black community in this country. The Church finds itself in a situation where it is the best continuing, organized entity in the Black community for the acquisition and redevelopment of land, the building of business enterprises and the employment of people."*[17]

When Churches invest in their neighborhoods, the result is a rise in property values, less crime, and often more cooperation between those that live in the community and outside groups. Church-based business enterprises help rebuild a community's social infrastructure and provide such values-based services as child care, youth development, elder care, and substance abuse counseling. These activities tend to lead to improved schools, better public safety, and an enhanced quality of life. From this type of community economic development, everyone benefits, both within the community and without.

---

16 Sherman, Good News.
17 Lloyd Gite, "The New Agenda of the Black Church," Black Enterprise, Dec. 1993, 54-56.

Here are some other specific ways Churches can help nurture the economic landscape of their communities.

• Build educational projects that both support the local public schools and provide what the schools can't. Examples include preschools, after-school tutoring, ESL and literacy classes, libraries, and computer training.

• Create a job information center. Provide computers for public use. Offer workshops in resume writing, interviewing techniques, credit building, entrepreneurial skills, and job searching.

• Support business owners within the Church. Produce a business directory listing all businesses owned and/or managed by Church members; provide copies to members and the community.

• Explore the concept of micro-financing as a viable alternative to traditional loans.[18]

• Establish money management seminars in conjunction with local municipal offices, schools, and banks.

By furthering entrepreneurial systems, creating jobs, and allowing for organizational activities, employment and prosperity, trust as a form of social capital often refines economic efficiency. Francis Fukuyama has persuasively argued that a higher level of social trust correlates positively with economic development. A widening number of social theorists and economists hold that societies with high levels of trust and social capital enjoy far more dynamism, innovation, elasticity, and prosperity than those that have a weak

---

[18] This is an underexplored tool in North America. For more analysis of some fluent models, see Dowla, Asif & Dipal Barua, The Poor Always Pay Back: The Grameen II Story. (Bloomfield, CT: Kumarian Press Inc., 2006); Marguerite S. Robinson, The Microfinance Revolution (Washington D.C.: The World Bank, 2001).

civil society.[19] It has been widely accepted and demonstrated that social trust benefits the economy and that the low level of trust inhibits economic growth. By entering as congregations into opportunities to transform our communities, we curtail our personal preoccupations with style, status, and success, embodying instead the Kingdom values of care, connectedness, concern, and collective responsibility that are so vital to the development and sustenance of authentically democratic community and peoplehood.

---

19 Trust is the emotional expectation that arises within a community of regular, honest, and cooperative behavior, based on commonly shared norms, on the part of other members of that community. Robert D. Putnam, Robert D., "Bowling Alone: America's Declining Social Capital," Journal of Democracy 6:1, Jan. 1995, 65–78. doi:10.1353/jod.1995.0002. http://xroads.virginia.edu/~HYPER/DETOC/assoc/bowling.html. See also Putnam's book, Bowling Alone: The Collapse and Revival of American Community (NY: Simon and Schuster, 2001).

CHAPTER NINE

BIG MONEY AND THE NEW "JIM CROW"

"For I was hungry and you gave me something to eat, I was thirsty and you gave me something to drink, I was a stranger and you invited me in, I needed clothes and you clothed me, I was sick and you looked after me, I was in prison and you came to visit me." Then the righteous will answer him, "Lord, when did we see you hungry and feed you, or thirsty and give you something to drink? When did we see you a stranger and invite you in, or needing clothes and clothe you? When did we see you sick or in prison and go to visit you?" The King will reply, "Truly I tell you, whatever you did for one of the least of these brothers and sisters of mine, you did for me."

—Mt. 25:35-40

And we've come to think about the prison industrial complex as linked very much to slavery, as revealing the sediments and the vestiges of slavery, as providing evidence that the slavery we may have thought was abolished with the Thirteenth Amendment is still very much with us. It haunts us, especially in the form of this vast prison industrial complex, a prison system within the US that holds something like 2.5 million people, more people in prison than anywhere else in the world, more people per capita, as well. ...And that's really only because of the disproportionate number

of Black people and people of color whose lives have been claimed by the prison system.
—Angela Davis

The idea was that the outcasts should keep their distance or at worse have to pay their way into some kind of nearness to the

heart of the body politic. Jesus crossed those lines. He touched those people. He even implied that the kingdom was for such as those. This was especially scandalous when you had both Roman and temple state systems saying otherwise.
—Mark Lewis Taylor

LOCKDOWN AMERICA[1]

So far we have attempted to map how urban communities have struggled to keep pace with the rest of the country in the post-soul, post-civil rights era of American public life. The story is a familiar one: the disappearance of viable work opportunities and viable businesses, the severe backlash of a mainstream conservative culture of "law and order," the avalanche of drugs, the heightened surveillance, the dissolution of quality public education engines, the withdrawal of social amenities, and the rise of a reptilian culture of materialism have all combined to produce subpockets of alienated communities in urban America. It means that the people living in these subaltern communities are largely invisible and as a result regard government re-institutional programs as insensitive and repressive regimes. Elijah Anderson, one of North America's more perceptive and astute commentators, highlights the racially discriminatory practice and punitive policies that compound the cauldron of poverty in urban America:

---

[1] Taylor, Executed God. For Taylor, "Lockdown America" is a society perpetually imprisoned by its own creation, a reptilian culture of fear constantly biting off its own tail in order to survive. See also my review of his book in Andrews University Seminary Studies, v.41:1, Spring 2003, 152-154

Black people are prevented from moving because of housing discrimination and from commuting because of lack of public transit. As local neighborhoods become perceived as "Black," the remaining white people leave, city services decline, and police and other institutions abdicate their responsibility to protect residents and property. The neighborhoods develop a "second-class" status. Eventually there is a concentration of poor Blacks, as middle-class Blacks join the white residents in fleeing the area. In addition, social welfare is being eliminated and many job-training programs have been terminated, further exacerbating so many of the conditions alluded to above. [2]

A NATION OF LAWS BUT NOT JUSTICE

The recent Wall Street crisis and the widespread bungling of institutional funds brought the nation's economy to the brink of collapse. Here is an example provided by Wall Street on Parade:

The undisputed reality is that the shareholders of Citigroup would be holding worthless stock today were it not for the company's rescue by taxpayers during the Wall Street collapse five years ago. And yet, today, based on reports from coast to coast, the company is engaging in egregious abuses of struggling young college graduates who took out private student loans from Citibank. [3]

The above narrative serves as an example of the nefarious acts committed by corporate companies that threaten the political economies of North America and Europe. Though the justice

---

2 Elijah Anderson, "The Social Ecology of Youth Violence," Crime and Justice, Vol. 24, Youth Violence (1998), p. 66.
3 Pam Martens, "Why Isn't the Justice Department Investigating Citibank's Student Loan Scandal? (Part I)," September 10, 2013. http://wallstreetonparade.com/2013/09/why-isn%E2%80%99t-the-justice-department-investigating-citibank%E2%80%99s-student-loan-scandal-part-i/. The narrative gets murkier and more sinister: "As we reported in August 2012, Citigroup was showing serious strains in 2007 but the meltdown came the week of November 17, 2008. . . Just one month prior to this stock meltdown, the U.S. government through its Troubled Asset Relief Program (TARP) had injected $25 billion into Citigroup on October 28, 2008. With a market cap of $20.5 billion on Friday, November 21, 2008, the U.S. taxpayer effectively owned this company lock, stock and barrel."

department conducted several investigations and levied billions of dollars in fines to guilty parties, not one person held responsible has gone to jail.

Judge Jed Rakoff of the Federal District Court in Manhattan has persuasively argued in a recent essay in The New York Review of Books that government legal agents have been slow in prosecuting Wall Street bosses because some top government officials may be found worthy of blame. He argues:

> But what I am suggesting is that the government was deeply involved, from beginning to end, in helping create the conditions that could lead to such fraud, and that this would give a prudent prosecutor pause in deciding whether to indict a CEO who might, with some justice, claim he was only doing what he fairly believed the government wanted him to do.[4]

Accounts abound of closed-door manipulations between government officials and banking executives that left the American taxpayer footing the bill for a $700 billion bailout. The average citizen now believes that there are two Americas: one rich and one poor, a two-tiered system of laws, one of which exists for rich whites and the other for poor people of color, largely male, who serve mandatory sentences for petty crimes such marijuana possession. People of color are seldom recipients of such legal grace and political favors. As Jesse Jackson once said, when a crime is committed, "The rich go to Yale, and the poor go to jail."

A NATION OF JAILS?

Perhaps the most alarming development of this complex age of deindustrialization is the rise of the prison industrial complex.

---

4 Capitol Report," Market Watch, The Wall Street Journal, Dec. 20, 2013. http://blogs.marketwatch.com/capitolreport/2013/12/20/federal-judges-take-on-why-no-wall-street-execs-have-been-prosecuted-for-fraud-during-crisis/

The saga of our age is that American systemic racial coding over-determines how colored men are perceived, represented, and tracked in this system of lockdown America. In an important essay detailing the political culture that surrounds the racialization of the judicial system, historian Paul Street argues that:

> *It is undeniable that the race to incarcerate is having a profoundly negative effect on Black communities. Equally undeniable is the fact that Black incarceration rates reflect deep racial bias in the criminal justice system and the broader society. Do the cheerleaders of "get tough" crime and sentencing policy really believe that African-Americans deserve to suffer so disproportionately at the hands of the criminal justice system? There is a vast literature showing that structural, institutional, and cultural racism and severe segregation by race and class are leading causes of inner-city crime. Another considerable body of literature shows that Blacks are victims of racial bias at every level of the criminal justice system, from stop, frisk, and arrest to prosecution, sentencing, release, and execution. These disparities give legitimacy to the movement of ex-offender groups for the expungement of criminal and prison records for many nonviolent offenses, especially in cases where ex-convicts have shown an earnest desire to "go straight."* [5]

Urban men are being incarcerated in record numbers. According to Demico Boothe, out of 10.4 million Black men in America, nearly 1.5 million are in prison or jail, and 3.5 million are currently or have been previously on probation or parole. According to the Common Sense for Drug Policy Institute, Black males were six times and Hispanic males 2.5 times more likely to be imprisoned than white males In 2012. Hispanic males ages 18 to 19 were more than three times as likely as white males of the same age to be imprisoned, while all other age groups were at least twice as likely as white

---

5 Paul Street, "Race, Prison, and Poverty —History Is A Weapon." http://www.historyisaweapon.com/defcon1/streeracpripov.html Demico Boothe, Why Are So Many Black Men in Prison? (U.S.: Full Surface Publishing, 2007).

males to be serving a prison sentence. Black males had imprisonment rates at least four times those of white males in all age groups.[6] The U.S. prison industry disproportionately shapes the life chances of an unusual amount of American citizens, especially Americans of color. For researchers like Boothe, the prison industry has become "a predator industry in the lives of African-American men."[7] Michelle Alexander calls the prison-industrial complex "the new Jim Crow." TV producer David Simon points out that "we are the country that jails more of our population than any other state on the globe, more [even] than totalitarian states."[8]

The many young men who reside in areas of concentrated urban poverty are mired in a cauldron of discrimination, unemployment, violence, crime, prison, and early death. This toxic mixture has given rise to wider stereotypes that limit the social capital of all young Black males. A huge slice of the 13 million persons locked away in American prisons are incarcerated for petty crimes that could be addressed through other less dehumanizing practices. Furthermore, it is not clear that the billion-dollar prison industry has secured a reduction in crime or made American neighborhoods safer.[9] Urban communities are disproportionately affected by the large numbers of men and women being shunted off to prison. According to Gary Highsmith, of the Yale-New Haven Teachers' Institute,

---

6 Drug War facts, "Race and Prison." http://www.drugwarfacts.org/cms/Race_and_Prison#sthash.ry6frWPe.dpbs.
7 Michelle Alexander, "The New Jim Crow: How the War on Drugs Gave Birth to a Permanent American Underclass," March 8, 2010. http://www.huffingtonpost.com/michelle-alexander/the-new-jim-crow-how-the_b_490386.html
8 David Simon in an interview with Bill Moyers, Jan. 31, 2014. http://billmoyers.com/episode/david-simon-on-america-as-a-horror-show/. David Simon is an American journalist and a writer/producer of the HBO series "The Wire" and "Treme." He is the author of Homicide: A Year on the Killing Streets(Boston: Houghton Mifflin, 1991) and The Corner: A Year in the Life of an Inner-City Neighborhood (NY: Broadway Books, 1997) with Ed Burns.
9 "Confronting Confinement," sponsored by the Vera Institute of Justice, a New York think tank, adds an eminent voice to the view that the recent boom in imprisonment has not always made Americans safer, even as violent crime has dropped. The report draws on hundreds of experts, including corrections officers, inmates, psychiatrists, policymakers, scholars and religious leaders. It paints a dispiriting portrait of incarceration in the United States, and contends that a high price is paid for poor policy and implementation, in dollars and anguish alike. Each year, the United States spends an estimated $60 billion on corrections.

The fact of the matter is that poor people, and especially poor Blacks, are convicted of crime more often, although there is no substantial relationship between social class and the commission of crimes. There is, however, a marked relationship between class and conviction for crime. In short, the fact that half or more of the 50 percent of the persons arrested for crimes of personal violence, and that 40 to 50 percent of all prisoners in jails and penitentiaries are Black says nothing at all about the criminality of Black people. And that an even higher proportion of persons arrested are poor and imprisoned sheds no light whatever on the criminality of the poor. These facts only identify the objects of police and court activity. There are law violators and there are law violators; one kind gets arrested, the other kind is usually left alone. It is not disingenuous to conclude, then, that those left alone are almost always White and/or wealthy. For in America, Whites clearly benefit from White-skin privilege. Conversely, Blacks appear to suffer from Black-skin punishment. [10]

There are several features that characterize the relationship of the prison-industrial complex to urban communities.

1. The prison-industrial complex signifies the breakdown of the family, the neighborhood, and a host of productive relationships.[11]

2. Racially coded language feeds mainstream suspicion of communities of color and fuels the legal and political engines that established mainstream acceptance for the industry.

3. The political slogans of law and order incite mainstream resentment of the gains of the Civil Rights era and the human rights movement that helped people of color.

---
10 Gary Highsmith,"Black Skin, White Justice: Race Matters in the Criminal Justice System." http://www.yale.edu/ynhti/curriculum/units/1996/1/96.01.10.x.html
11 Jamie Fellner, "US Addiction to Incarceration Puts 2.3 Million in Prison." Human Rights Watch(November 30, 2006). http://www.hrw.org/news/2006/11/30/us-addiction-incarceration-puts-23-million-prison. Retrieved 2007-06-02.

4. The prison-industrial complex reduces social and intellectual capital, in that a sizeable segment of the population is precluded from the work force and is therefore bereft of gaining the requisite skills to contribute to civil society.

5. The system of justice itself takes on huge burdens. The results of systemic failure often lead to increased social and financial costs for private citizens and the government as a whole.

6. The prison-industrial complex is inextricable linked to big money and big government.

7. The prison-industrial complex leads to de-industrialization, loss of jobs, and the dilapidated school systems.

8. The prison-industrial complex exaggerates the image of an outlaw culture among urban youth and leads to the demonization of Black youth in general within the broader society.

9. The prison-industrial complex points to a lack of compassion that spreads from governmental agencies through families and religious organizations, and ultimately into the Church.

10. The prison-industrial complex highlights the connection between the war on drugs, the war on the middle class, and the war on education.

In her fascinating analysis, *The New Jim Crow: Mass Incarceration in the Age of Colorblindness*, legal scholar Michelle Alexander shows that the last 40 years in North America have seen the incarceration of Black Americans at a record rate. This is largely attributable to federal and state agencies' "war on drugs," a program that has unfairly targeted poor inner city residents. Further, Alexander contends that although Jim Crow laws are no longer in effect, millions of Americans, especially African Americans and members of other marginalized communities, are tarred and feathered by the criminal justice system. Imprisoned at a young age, they are branded as felons and denied the basic rights and opportunities that would allow them to become productive.[12] "People are swept into the criminal justice system—particularly in poor communities of color—at very early ages . . . typically for fairly minor, nonviolent crimes," Alexander says in an interview with Fresh Air's Dave Davies.[13] She continues:

> [Young Black males are] shuttled into prisons, branded as criminals and felons, and then when they're released, they're relegated to a permanent second-class status, stripped of the very rights supposedly won in the civil rights movement—like the right to vote, the right to serve on juries, the right to be free of legal discrimination and employment, and access to education and public benefits. Many of the old forms of discrimination that we supposedly left behind during the Jim Crow era are suddenly legal again, once you've been branded a felon.[14]

RETURNING CITIZENS OR CASTAWAYS?

Each year the nation's prisons and jails release more than 11.5 million inmates.[15] When these men and women present themselves as candidates for dignified work, they are routinely turned down by employers. Denied the opportunity to be productive citizens, they are left by the wayside.

---

12 Michelle Alexander, The New Jim Crow: Mass Incarceration in the Age of Colorblindness (NY: The New Press, 2012).
13 "Legal Scholar: Jim Crow Still Exists in America," January 16, 2012. http://www.npr.org/2012/01/16/145175694/legal-scholar-jim-crow-still-exists-in-america
14 Ibid.
15 Results from the 2010 NSDUH: Summary of National Findings. http://www.samhsa.gov/data/nsduh/2k10nsduh/2k10results.htm

The prison industrial complex, according to Princeton sociologist Bruce Western, has "large and enduring effects on job prospects of ex-convicts."[16]

The criminal records of young parolees can circumscribe their chances of securing meaningful employment decades after their return to civil society. According to Paul Street, "Since incarceration rates are especially high among those with the least power in the labor market (young and unskilled minority men)," going to prison is a key indicator that a person will not enter the ranks of the working and middle class.[17] The American dream for so many of these young men caught in the toxic cycle of discrimination, violence, mis-education, and unemployment quickly turns into a nightmare.

There are several studies of the hardships endured by citizens trying to negotiate reentry into society and explore the possibilities of decent work and well-being. A 2002 study showed that among nearly 275,000 prisoners released in 1994, 67.5 percent were rearrested within three years and 51.8 percent were back in prison.[18] Upon emergence from life behind bars, many ex-inmates hunt for the social acceptance and civic services that the average citizen takes for granted. Jobs are hard to obtain. Housing often proves difficult. And society in general has shifted.

---

16 Bruce Western, as quoted by Paul Street, "History is a Weapon: Race, Prison and Poverty." http://www.historyisaweapon.com/defcon1/streeracpripov.html
17 Paul Street, "History is a Weapon."
18 Patrick A. Langan and David J. Levin, David J., "Recidivism of Prisoners Released in 1994." Bureau of Justice Statistics. June 2, 2002. http://bjs.gov/content/pub/pdf/rpr94.pdf. See also Roy Walmsley, "World Prison Population List (10th edition)," International Center for Prison Studies. http://www.prisonstudies.org/sites/prisonstudies.org/files/resources/downloads/wppl_10.pdf This research is consistent with numerous experimental studies suggesting that the employment prospects of job applicants with criminal records are far worse than the chances of persons who have never been convicted or imprisoned. According to a New York Times report, "Even when paroled inmates are able to find jobs, they earn only half as much as people of the same social and economic background who have not been incarcerated." As quoted in Paul Street, "History is a Weapon."

Many times ex-inmates are asked to pay back their court costs and can have their wages garnished up to 100 percent.[19] This makes it impossible for these men and women to earn a living. Depending on the amount of time spent away, ex-inmates experience profound changes. And if they come from communities of concentrated poverty, they must navigate the vagaries of communities that have gotten even worse. Chaplain Jerry Cabluck, who leads a ministry that helps ex-convicts gain meaningful lives upon leaving prison, says, "When an incarcerated person is released, the first thing that happens is they encounter prostitutes, alcohol, drugs—sin and temptation right in front of them. The Lord's calling on my heart is to help ex-offenders learn basic life skills and provide a support network to help them resist the temptation to fall back into old, self-defeating lifestyles."[20] Ex-inmates typically return to urban areas lacking not only the basic tools for getting around, but also the coping skills required for life in the city. According to the Reentry Policy Council, a project of the Council of State Governments Justice Center:[21]

- Three of four offenders released from prisons have a substance abuse problem. Only 10 percent in state prisons receive treatment during incarceration.

---

19 Michele Alexander on Moyers and Company, Dec. 20, 2013. http://billmoyers.com/segment/michelle-alexander-locked-out-of-the-american-dream/. Before their prison experience many of these individuals suffered from financial, educational and cultural disadvantages. Without sufficient support from family and Church they are easily exposed to situations in which their lack of skills and resources leave them with few if any options. See also "The Inclusion of Ex Offenders within the Christian Community," Diocese of Oxford. Though from the U.K., much in this report is also true of the problems returning citizens face in North America. http://www.oxford.anglican.org/mission-ministry/faith-in-action/criminal-justice/the-inclusion-of-ex-offenders-within-the-christian-community/.
20 Jerry Cabluck in "Ministries Help Ex-offenders Re-enter Society Beyond Prison," by Ken Camp. The Baptist Standard, Mar 11, 2013. https://www.baptiststandard.com/news/texas/14841-ministries-help-ex-offenders-re-enter-society-beyond-prison.
21 The website of The National Reentry Resource Center provides education, training, and technical assistance to states, tribes, territories, local governments, service providers, non-profit organizations, and corrections institutions working on prisoner reentry. http://csgjusticecenter.org/jc/category/reentry/nrrc/

- More than one in three reports some physical or mental disability.

- More than half—55 percent—have at least one child under age 18 who depends on the ex-offender for financial support.

- Only one-third participated in educational programs in prison, and barely more than one-fourth (27 percent) received vocational training.

THE PRISON INDUSTRIAL CRISIS

The prison system is one of the fastest growing industries in America. From 1980 to 2013 the number of inmates in federal custody swelled by 800 percent. More than 60 percent of the people in prison are colored. In 2012 the budget request for the Federal Bureau of Prisons (BOP) was a staggering $6.9 billion.[22]

According to the Baltimore Sun, this has not yielded positive results.[23] The article goes on to say that budget deficits have forced many governmental agencies review to the high cost of prison maintenance.[24]

---

[22] "The American Prison System is Overcrowded," The Telescope, Palomar College, Oct 3, 2013. http://www2.palomar.edu/telescope/2013/10/03/the-american-prison-system-is-overcrowded/. The article goes on to argue that "the average low-security prisoner incurs $25,000 in costs annually. By current figures from the U.S. Department of Agriculture, that's enough to feed a family of four for over a year and a half. There are better places to put our hard-earned dollars than into the inefficiencies of the prison system. Education, healthcare and the $17 trillion U.S. debt quickly comes to mind. But what inefficiencies are we talking about? Today, the central issue lies with drug sentencing laws. According to an August report by the BOP, nearly 50 percent of federal prisoners are behind bars for drug offenses. The majority of these prisoners are non-violent offenders who, due to the immense overload of the prison system, will not receive the help they need."
[23] "Prison overload," The Baltimore Sun, Aug 19, 2003. http://articles.baltimoresun.com/2003-08-19/news/0308190328_1_prison-systems-nonviolent-drug-offenders-number-of-prisoners.
[24] See also "New Prison Statistics: Nation's Use of Incarceration on the Rise Again," Justice Policy Institute, July 25, 2003.http://www.prisonpolicy.org/scans/jpi/new_prison_stats.pdf. "The prison population and budget figures—taken together—should be setting off alarm bells in state capitols," says Jason Ziedenberg, Director of Policy and Research for the Justice Policy Institute. "As legislators are struggling to fund education, health care, and stave off spending cuts, many are continuing to choose to pay for an expensive justice system that damages communities, and does not produce safe, healthy neighborhoods."

In the face of this systemic overload, many government agencies have opted for early release programs. This means that many communities—and the Churches within them—will have to prepare for the influx of returning citizens. As American Baptist Home Mission Societies rhetorically asks, "Are we prepared to deal with the conflicts caused by having victims and perpetrators entering the same place of worship?"[25]

THE CHURCH: GRACE-OFFERING FATHER OR GRUDGE-HOLDING BROTHER?

To many middle-class Americans, ex-inmates are abnormal, sub-human creatures. But those who are returning from prison need help, and Churches and Christian organizations can provide that help in the form of resources for jobs, education, transportation, and basic life skills. However, the most important thing the Church can provide is a place of acceptance and affirmation. According to Sie Davis, a returned citizen and Church planter who leads a residential ministry in Dallas to help ex-offenders, "There's a transition in the mind when a person goes into prison—moving from this big old world to go live in a little cell and never go more than two or three miles for years at a time."[26]

DEAD AND ALIVE: THE PARABLE OF THE LOST SON

> *There was a man who had two sons. The younger one said to his father, "Father, give me my share of the estate." So he divided his property between them. Not long after that, the younger son got together all he had, set off for a distant country and there squandered his wealth in wild living. After he had spent everything, there was a severe famine in that whole country, and he began to be in need. So he went and hired himself out to a*

---

[25] "Prisoner Re-entry and Aftercare Ministry," ABHMS. http://www.abhms.org/justice_ministries/prisoner_re-entry/
[26] Sie Davis, in "Ministries Help Ex-offenders Re-enter Society Beyond Prison," by Ken Camp. The Baptist Standard, Mar 11, 2013. https://www.baptiststandard.com/news/texas/14841-ministries-help-ex-offenders-re-enter-society-beyond-prison

citizen of that country, who sent him to his fields to feed pigs. He longed to fill his stomach with the pods that the pigs were eating, but no one gave him anything. When he came to his senses, he said, "How many of my father's hired servants have food to spare, and here I am starving to death! I will set out and go back to my father and say to him: 'Father, I have sinned heaven and against you. I am no longer worthy to be called your son make me like one of your hired servants.'" So he got up and went to his father. But while he was still a long way off, his father saw him and was filled with compassion for him; he ran to his son, threw his arms around him and kissed him. The son said to him, "Father, I have sinned against heaven and against you. I am no longer worthy to be called your son." But the father said to his servants, "Quick! Bring the best robe and put it on him. Put a ring on his finger and sandals on his feet. Bring the fattened calf and kill it. Let's have a feast and celebrate. For this son of mine was dead and is alive again; he was lost and is found." So they began to celebrate. Meanwhile, the older son was in the field. When he came near the house, he heard music and dancing. So he called one of the servants and asked him what was going on. "Your brother has come," he replied, "and your father has killed the fattened calf because he has him back safe and sound." The older brother became angry and refused to go in. So his father went out and pleaded with him. But he answered his father, "Look! All these years I've been slaving for you and never disobeyed your orders. Yet you never gave me even a young goat so I could celebrate with my friends. But when this son of yours who has squandered your property with prostitutes comes home, you kill the fattened calf for him!" "My son," the father said, "you are always with me, and everything I have is yours. But we had to celebrate and be glad, because this brother of yours was dead and is alive again; he was lost and is found." (Luke 15:11-32)

When Jesus told this story to those gathered around Him, what must have been most astonishing to them was the forgiving heart of the father. Upon the son's return he is met with an unusual and unimaginable welcome. His return inspires his father to inaugurate a reunion, a celebration that stands in stark contrast to his deepest fears. This is grace come alive. Rather than punishment and relegation to the basement of his familial hierarchy, the son enjoys a reception of rare hospitality and refinement. His home serves as the theatre of embrace and exaltation rather than prevarication and punishment. This unexpected gesture chokes our narrow understanding of fairness. The father's compassion, the main ingredient in the story, represents the undying love that God the Creator has for His wayward children. Even though during his journey the son's mind was not on his father, the father's mind was on the son. Paul said, "While we were yet sinners Christ died for us" (Rom. 5:8). Love cannot live a single moment without focusing on its object. Most hearers would expect the father to exact some punitive measure against the son. The text speaks of no such thing. There is no mention of remediation or probation—simply the compassionate spirit of a father longing for reunion and reconciliation. The father is the governing character of the drama whose arc rises from alienation to affirmation. In the wake of his departure the younger son left a trail of acrimony and annoyance. By seizing his inheritance he breached the canons of trust and thus reached the point of no return. Jesus' story is meant to invert the received wisdom of the day. True mercy is countercultural. Grace is the epicenter of the new community of moral flourishing and compassionate living that ushers in the reign of God. Jesus' discourse, then, ambushes as much as it embraces. It startles as much as it saves. For Jesus, the master and author of the story, there is no sin, no violation of the covenant relationship, no descent into recklessness, no accusation so deep that it cannot be taken up in the loving arms of a heavenly Father. Compassion means we go against our carnal inclinations. Grace rises over punishment. Joy rises above vengeance. Compassion takes the place of crime and punishment.

But not everyone shares the zeal and felicity of the choral blessing. The eldest son, upon hearing the rising rhythms of the merry-makers, launches an inquiry, only to be told that the party is held in honor of his brother who, in the elder brother's mind, still represents abject fallenness and failure, not healthy reformation and honorable reunion. Playing the role of the great despoiler, chafing at the celebratory stipend given to his younger sibling, he challenges his father. To his deeply retributive and yet all too human mind, justice has not been done. For him the old man's actions are morally treasonable and therefore indefensible. The resoluteness and intensity of the younger sibling's repentance is equaled only by the ferocity of the older brother's disregard for him and contempt for his father. The older brother's self-obsession leaves little room for reunion let alone compassion. It is revealing that he refuses to even set eyes on this forsaken brother who he assumed he would never see again. He remains outside, refusing to attend the party. And this is what unforgiveness does: it banishes us from our own home and from what God has made rightfully ours. The older brother had come to enjoy the prosperity but had not learned the humility and beauty of being with his father. In all those intervening years the father's glad wisdom and heartfelt grace had never penetrated his emotional armor.

Why reward wanton mindlessness with such lavish favor? the older brother asks. "This son of yours has squandered his father's money on illicit sexual escapades." The elder brother's attitude, not unlike many Churchgoers today, is self-righteous and haughty. For many Christians, compassion, born of deep humility, is largely absent from the notion or practice of worship. They may be physically close to the altar of authentic worship, but spiritually they are nowhere near it. While they probe deep into the lives of others, they never fully give themselves to the God of salvation. Ingratitude, the lack of a deep-felt appreciation for who God is and what God has done, is a serious disease in many congregations. While the image of the younger brother may be one of immaturity, the picture of the older brother is a profound ingratitude. All this time the seething sentiments of rebellion lay dormant, quietly suppressed into the deepest crevices of his soul, only to find an outlet upon an occasion saved for grace and reunion. Yet the father is fixed on mercy. He says tenderly to this oldest son, "My son, you are always with me, and everything I have is yours. But we had to celebrate and be glad, because this brother of yours was dead and is alive again; he was lost and is found."

God forgives. That is the meaning of grace. God shows his forgiveness through an extravagant, unbridled compassion. Jesus provided the tale of God's boundless love for a suffering and miscreant humanity. His answer to this human predicament of weakness and woe is grace, the unleashing of undying love to provide for human prodigals what they so clearly cannot provide for themselves: a way out of their self-sanctioned dungeons.

GRACE EXTENDED: WHAT THE COMMUNITY CAN DO

In his essay, "Correcting the System of Unequal Justice," James Bell, founder and executive director of the W. Haywood Burns Institute, provides a list of steps to help communities address the systemic unfairness rampant in American society in general and the U.S. penal system specifically. Here are some of his most critical ideas:

• Hold leaders and elected officials responsible and demand that they change current policy.

• Form adult clubs in the neighborhood to plan activities and create safe houses where children can hang out when parents are not home. Tell parents when you see children behaving in dangerous ways.

- Support children whose parents are incarcerated.[27]

In addition, there are many things that congregations and individual Christians can do to alleviate the challenges that returning citizens face: [28]

- Focus heavily on building excellent youth departments.

- Establish male and female rite of passage programs centered on the possibilities, beauty, and dignity of urban youth.

- Focus on developing relevant ministries for men and women.

- Educate the congregation on reentry culture and programs.

- Establish prayer circles and ministries to help those who are returning.

- Volunteer at places that support returning citizens.

- Establish connections with mental health facilities that can provide assistance with psychological and sexual issues that returning citizens face.

- Develop sound and fair neighborhood policing programs.

- Build alliances and coalitions to create small businesses and jobs for returning citizens.

- Develop networks between returning citizens and mentors.

---

27 See James Bell's introductory essay in The Covenant with Black America (Chicago: Third World Press, 2006), 55.
28 See more at "The Inclusion of Ex Offenders within the Christian Community," Diocese of Oxford.http://www.oxford.anglican.org/mission-ministry/faith-in-action/criminal-justice/the-inclusion-of-ex-offenders-within-the-christian-community/.

- Provide support groups for families who have been impacted by the return of an incarcerated family member.

- Create ministries for prison visits.

Returning citizens are Americans that do not benefit from the American tradition of the "second chance." These opportunities presuppose moral investment and emotional involvement, an appreciation of human dignity and wisdom, and trust in the social bonds and accountability. Such currencies are alarmingly scarce in the common cultural marketplace. The Church is often victim and villain in this litany of social error. So often we cannot afford to see our neighbor, for this causes unbearable dissonance in the precinct of the soul. This narcissistic spirit requires that the soul turn inward and elevate itself at the expense of others. The Church stands as a community built on the denial of these twin enemies of faith: narcissism and mistrust. To this end, in the eyes of the world the Church must commit suicide. It must bear its cross. Without this it has nothing of value to give to the world.

CHAPTER TEN

QUILTING HOPE:

THE CHANGING FACE OF PARENTING AND FAMILIES

Wherever His Spirit appears, the oppressed gather fresh courage; for He announced the good news that fear, hypocrisy, and hatred, the three hounds of hell that track the trail of the disinherited, need have no dominion over them.
—Howard Thurman, Jesus and the Disinherited

The family remains the child's first community; parents are their foremost teachers. Parenting is not only crucial to personal psychic well-being, but a key indicator for the type of human a child will become. The love, discipline, and support of loving parents are absolutely necessary to guide children through the stages of life. Without this guidance, children are shipwrecked and society is lost at sea. Yet while many desire children, the ethic of parenting is not in vogue. Parenting means sacrifice. It requires maturity, selflessness, and the capacity to put off one's own wants. In short, parenting means it's not about you.

Added to this challenge is the fact that well-paying jobs are disappearing in many urban centers, and this affects the parenting power of many working-class and poor people, specifically fathers of color. Men who feel unable to express themselves in a meaningful occupation or creative vocation or who feel unable to secure material resources for a decent living tend to have higher registers of anxiety, depression, and anger. Forced to choose between unemployment, homelessness, crime, and the diminishing supply of poor paying jobs, such men feel suffocated and worn down.

The decline in the health of home, Church, and school can often be traced back to the breakdown of the family, the disintegration of marriages, the redefinition of Black manhood, and the disappearance of Black fatherhood.

There are still many African-American fathers who have shown tremendous competency in the area of parenting: staying at home, taking care of the details, spending time reading, working on homework, doing laundry, going to parent-teacher association meetings, monitoring sleepovers, going to sporting events, or coaching a sports team. Most of this is work typically considered the domain of the female parent. However, fathers who are involved in the lives of their children often feel better about themselves than those who do not.

In a now classic essay by Arlie Russell Hochschild and Anne Machung, the authors note the following of men who share "the second shift":

> *In the end caring for children in the most important part of the second shift, and the effects of a man's care or his neglect will show up again and again through time—in the child as a child,*

in the child as an adult, and probably also in the child's own approach to fatherhood, and in generations of fathers to come.[1]

I have been talking more about parenting specifically rather than the family in general because the reality is that in many American families a parent is absent. This does not necessarily mean, however, that children who are in one-parent homes or are raised by people other than their biological parents have missed out on the love and support that a family brings. Love and support show up in families that are structured all sorts of ways. Are we in the Church aware and supportive of families that don't meet the traditional model? Do we listen to their voices and stories, especially in the context of urban living, in order to know how best to serve them?

UNSUNG: THE PLIGHT AND PROMISE OF SINGLE URBAN MOTHERS

> *I am not the "typical" single mother, but then there is no typical single mother any more than there is a typical mother. It is, in fact, our fantasies and crude stereotypes of this "typical single mother" that get in the way of a more rational, open-minded understanding of the variety and richness of different kinds of families.*
>
> —Katie Roiphe, New York Times

The unfolding tale of urban America is a tale of God's people negotiating the howling wilderness. The unsung person in contemporary North America is the single parent, especially the single mother—hardworking, intrepid, dauntless, and who against the odds makes her mark on the world and raises her children in fair circumstances. These women are living symbols of the pressure and promise of the future of the city. In their lives we see stories

---

[1] Arlie Russell Hochschild and Anne Machung, The Second Shift (New York: Penguin Books, 2003), 249.

of the resistance and resourcefulness of the human spirit and of God's unfailing love. We see courage to weather in the storm—come what may! As the ethicist Keri Day, author of Unfinished Business, has shown, many urban women live in isolated pockets of poverty or semi-poverty. Their fragile access to a living wage, childcare, healthcare, and legal aid compounds their social remoteness and circumscribes their chances of ever emerging from this downward spiral of poverty.[2] Yet through their witness we find beauty in place of ashes. We see that hope has come to the city, an unborn hope that refuses to die.

CHILDREN AND SINGLE MOTHERS: THE STATE OF URBAN AMERICA

A report from Politico states:

> *Today, a quarter of American children live in single-parent homes. This comes with a huge economic burden: Over 20 percent of children raised in single-parent families end up in long-term poverty, compared with just two percent of those raised in two-parent homes. Over the last 50 years, the rise in out-of-wedlock births and divorces has been dramatic.* [3]

The statistics are staggering. We now live in a country in which 53 percent of the babies born to women under 30 are born to unmarried mothers.[4]

---

[2] Keri Day, Unfinished Business: Black Women, the Black Church, and the Struggle to Thrive in America (Orbis Books, 2002). For a subtle examination of how systemic forces conspire to demean and degrade women of color, see Emilie Townes, Womanist Ethics and the Cultural Production of Evil (Palgrave Macmillan, 2006). See also Katie Cannon's Black Womanist Ethic (Wipf and Stock, 2006).

[3] Ian Bremmer, "5 Stats That Explained the World This Week." Politico Magazine, April 27, 2014 http://www.politico.com/magazine/story/2014/04/5-stats-that-explained-the-world-this-week-106063.html#ixzz34Yyb65YY

[4] Katie Roiphe, "In Defense of Single Motherhood," NY Times Online, August 11, 2012 http://www.nytimes.com/2012/08/12/opinion/sunday/in-defense-of-single-motherhood.html. In the United States, 31 percent of Black children have both a mother and a father in the home; 53 percent have only a mother present; 7 percent have only a father present; and 9 percent have neither parent present. At 28 percent, the percentage of white children in single-parent homes has grown to exceed the figure that originally caused Sen. Daniel Moynihan's consternation for Black families in 1965. In fact, the U.S. has nearly 4 million more white children in single-parent households than Black children. If white families did not have children out of wedlock,

Today more children are being raised in households with unmarried parents than at any other time in our nation's history. Even as the total number of American households with children increased by 160,000, the number of two-parent households decreased by 1.2 million. Marriage has declined most significantly among the "moderately educated" and the poor. It is simply no longer seen as a necessary "fact of life." Between 1960 and 2005, the rate of unwed childbearing increased sevenfold, from 5.3 percent of all births to 36.8 percent. One survey finds that the average unwed mother "is more likely to be white than Black, and more likely to be an adult than a teenager."[5]

The world of single parenthood is thorny and intricate. It is quite easy for mainstream commentators to paint the members of this group with a broad assumptive brush. As Katie Roiphe has shown, many academic studies of the demographic of single mothers oversimplify issues and stories, reducing the complexities of forces and factors, motives and moods that shape people's lives. What we need are stories that explore how complex people negotiate challenges in their lives en route to deeper self-understanding and greater self-betterment. There exists no single narrative, viewpoint, or fiction that can and should shape the Church's understanding of the broad and fluctuating field of single parenthood. This is especially so with regard to urban dwellers. Single parenthood is multifaceted and multi-layered.

---

divorce or abandon their children, the total population of children in single-parent and no-parent homes would reduce by nearly 40 percent. By comparison, Black people account for 25 percent of the total population of children in single-parent homes. The percentage of Black children in single-parent homes is more than twice the percentage of whites. However, in the context of social impact, total incidents are unequivocally more important than within group percentages. See also Kristen Andersen, "The number of US children living in single-parent homes has nearly doubled in 50 years: Census Data," LifeSite News, January 4, 2013. http://www.lifesitenews.com/news/the-number-of-children-living-in-single-parent-homes-has-nearly-doubled-in

5 Pew Research, Social and Demographic Trends. http://www.pewsocialtrends.org/2010/05/06/the-new-demography-of-american-motherhood/

The background and life experiences of single mothers defy easy categorization or classification. These parents are as different in temperament, background, experience, education, and religious outlook as one can imagine. Some women's husbands have been murdered, have died of natural causes, or have been killed while serving in the military. Some women choose to have children outside of marriage; others are divorced, separated, or have husbands or partners in jail. Katie Roiphe points out that in fact women move in and out of singleness: married parents break apart, men and women live together without marrying, spouses or partners die, romantic attachments form and dissolve.[6]

STIGMAS THAT SINGLE MOTHERS MUST COMBAT

> *I certainly do feel different, you know, a little bit out of the norm at school when I'm dropping him off or, you know, just among parents at play dates and things like that. There is this sense, which I think kind of reminds me a little bit of the way my parents, who were, you know, children of the Depression, they used to discourage me from playing with the children of divorced parents, as if, you know, I would just go over there and immediately start dropping acid because they were divorced parents, you know.[7]*

The above quote highlights the stereotypes and negative feelings our society transfers onto single mothers. Here is a short list of assumptions that lead to misconceptions:

- Single parents are irresponsible teenagers.

- Singles parents are leeches on the system.

- Single parents/single mothers are incapable of raising productive children on their own.

---
6 Rophie.
7 Talk of the Nation, "For Single Mothers, Stigma Difficult To Shake." NPR, February 24, 2011. http://www.npr.org/2011/02/24/134031175/For-Single-Mothers-Stigma-Difficult-To-Shake.

- Single mothers are drama queens.

- Single mothers are emotionally isolated.

- Single parents require more support than they give.

- Single parents are poor and uneducated.

- The children of single parents are at a psychological and social disadvantage.

- Single implies abandoned, burdensome, broken, incomplete, poorer, inferior, and weak.

- Single parents are solely or at least primarily responsible for their disadvantages.

A society creates and maintains social distinctions that shape its internal self-definition and underpin its social hierarchy. These social distinctions provide the semblance of emotional safety and help to structure positive expectations and the returns that follow. The struggle for power and prestige gives birth to struggles over identity, influence, place, and position. In these struggles, we often fail to protect the feelings and emotional nature of single parents. Perhaps it is because of a need to feel separate and distinct from others who we deem to be less than us. Perhaps it is because of the interesting dance we do with the media: we feed the media our assumptions and the media create images and feed them back to us. The trend toward stigmatizing those who are "different" seems to be undeniable.

The way our culture views women informs the way our culture views single mothers. Considerable gains in women's rights and resources and the expansion of their presence in public roles and institutions are undeniable. Yet entrenched cultural assumptions that have undergirded their marginalization and misrepresentation have proven hard to displace. The assumption goes like this: If woman's proper sphere is the home, and if children are not developing into responsible citizens, then it must be the woman's fault, either for abandoning the home by going into the workplace (the male domain) or for remaining in the home as a deficient (e.g., single and therefore incomplete) being. The underlying message is that women are responsible. If children don't reach their potential, women are to blame. Not men. The double-edged sword swings in both worlds, public and private, and everywhere in between. Let's ignore draconian social policy, let's overlook historical discrimination and confinement, and let's overlook anti-Black and anti-female cultural attitudes. Let's just blame all our ills on women. And as bell hooks has emphasized over and over again, it is not surprising that women are seen as inferior in a society in which people assess their worth and value by their capacity to control and dominate others.[8] It is not a huge leap then to view single motherhood as a symptom of the general decline and incivility that characterizes broader society.

Many single mothers resent the fact that people see them as leeches on society and not as productive, creative and successful agents of destiny. Sister Amanda says,

> I'm a single mom, and I actually have lent support and help to some married friends. Nobody writing these articles ever concedes the possibility that we might be anything but a leech on our buddies.[9]

---

[8] bell hooks, Ain't I a Woman: Black Woman and Feminism (Cambridge, Mass.: South End Press, 1999).
[9] "Single Motherhood: So Many Different Circumstances," Urban Mammas, March 2012 http://www.urbanmamas.com/urbanmamas/2012/03/single-motherhood-so-many-different-circumstances.html

In fact, those single mothers who have achieved successes in education and career on their own while raising their children are seldom recognized. Yet their struggles are no less real for being "hidden" behind financial stability. Sister Catherine is an example: After I became pregnant, I discovered that not only was my husband having an affair, the woman he was with was also pregnant. Their daughter is four months younger than my daughter. Our marriage did not survive his constant infidelities and that's how I became a single parent. The greatest sorrow I still experience is watching my [now adult] daughter gravitate to unhealthy relationships as she seems to seek love and acceptance that she did not receive from her father.[10]

Veronica is trying to negotiate her peculiar situation. She articulates the needs and concerns of quite few single mothers:

> *While I know I'm not at all alone, I don't feel I fit any of the categories. There seems to be good support for coupled and single moms, but there aren't many for those that were previously coupled and are trying to figure out the difficulties of co-parenting with an ex that can sometimes be quite challenging. In many ways, I think it's beneficial to have him around for my kids and for the "break" it provides, which full-time single parents don't have. However, it also offers many challenges and lots of stress trying to make decisions together when you're not together and not having any control over how he parents or what happens when your children aren't with you. I'd love to have a group of moms to support each other from this part of the spectrum as well.* [11]

To compound matters, single fathers are seldom scrutinized or stigmatized with the intensity directed toward single mothers. In

---

[10] Interview with Catherine, Thursday June 13, 2014, Palmer Theological Seminary, King of Prussia, PA.
[11] Comment by "Recently Separated and Struggling," March 20, 2012, on "Single Motherhood: so many different circumstances." Urban Mamas http://www.urbanmamas.com/urbanmamas/2012/03/single-motherhood-so-many-different-circumstances.html

fact, a large swath of the sociological literature that informs policy making sounds narrowly moralistic and crudely judgmental. No wonder these women are seen as a burden on the social system while other Americans who may also be victims of historical oppression, cultural degradation, and political exclusion tend to be viewed with sympathy and are therefore worthy to receive support or assistance. The national gaze upon single urban mothers reinforces and sustains a politics of exclusion and silence that is more punitive than ameliorative.

RADICAL COMPASSION AND COMPASSIONATE MINISTRY

> *A certain woman of the wives of the sons of the prophets cried out to Elisha, saying, "Your servant my husband is dead, and you know that your servant feared the LORD. And the creditor is coming to take my two sons to be his slaves." So Elisha said to her, "What shall I do for you? Tell me, what do you have in the house?" And she said, "Your maidservant has nothing in the house but a jar of oil." Then he said, "Go, borrow vessels from everywhere, from all your neighbors—empty vessels; do not gather just a few. And when you have come in, you shall shut the door behind you and your sons; then pour it into all those vessels, and set aside the full ones." So she went from him and shut the door behind her and her sons, who brought the vessels to her; and she poured it out. Now it came to pass, when the vessels were full, that she said to her son, "Bring me another vessel." And he said to her, "There is not another vessel." So the oil ceased. Then she came and told the man of God. And he said, "Go, sell the oil and pay your debt; and you and your sons live on the rest. (2 Kings 4:1-7)*

In this engaging interchange between the prophet Elisha and a widow who is being harassed by creditors, we glean some insights into a portable approach to missional creativity. The woman had been left with little social standing and few resources. She had no job, no trade, and no profession that would allow her to secure funds and provide for her family. She was thrown into a situation with no public assistance, no pension, no living will, and no family support system for her children.

Unable to meet the hefty final obligation, the grief-stricken single mother of two approaches Elisha. In a swift, singular act of pastoral care and empowerment, Elisha asks her what she has in the house. By so doing he demands from her a degree of responsibility and a personal investment in the program of her restoration, laying the groundwork for a creative partnership that seeks a practical solution to her problem. Her response is instructive: "I have nothing, save a bit of oil." No matter what our state is, we can still offer God something to work with. The widow participates in her deliverance with an act of personal investment, and the community participates by providing the empty jars. Elisha instructs her to pour her limited supply of oil in the jars that she has collected, and the oil multiplies—enough to fill every donated jar. Evidently a broader plan is at work. Elisha has invited the widow into a season of entrepreneurial promise. She may now begin a trade to free herself from debt and build a solid economic foundation for herself and her children.

The plight of the family in this story is symbolic of the tenuous way of life that defines much of urban America. The widow is both grieving and debt-ridden, a combination that breeds despair and dread for so many urban dwellers the world over. The fusion of depersonalization and systemic forces creates a canopy of crisis that compels investigation by anyone involved in God's deliverance of the disinherited and dispossessed. Other key lessons emerge from this seminal event. Since stewardship is a species of spiritual leadership, the representatives of God (clergy and lay) are called to serve the most vulnerable and victimized of society by meeting them where they are and forming credible bonds. Elisha listened to the woman's plea for merciful intervention before responding—a compassionate approach that sowed the seed of a creative partnership. In a world experiencing huge disparities in income equality, economic deprivation, and social fragmentation, the Church can serve as a co-worker with Christ as it stands in solidarity with the dispossessed. By developing "listening hearts" we can forge authentic relationships of shared investment and mutual accountability with those who would otherwise experience civil and psychic death.

The widow in this Old Testament story represents single urban mothers who are called to navigate a life that is "no crystal stair."[12] The demand for them to be stewards of our collective moral future is in no way lessened by the grim circumstances of their lives. As a servant of God, Elisha serves as a caretaker for the caregivers of our communal future. By being a vessel of hope, he extends God's grace to future generations, highlighting a radical act of hospitality that models the ethic of empowerment that the Church can extend to the most vulnerable in the community.

This story also sheds light on the indomitability of the human will. Our celebrity-crazed, Peter Pan culture of "affluenza"[13] has little patience for those who do not come with all the "bells and whistles." Hence those unfairly cast as tragic and truant by the mainstream are overlooked and ignored as possible instruments of inspiration, liberation, and regeneration. Yet God chose things the world considers foolish in order to shame those who think they are wise. And he chose things that are powerless to shame those who are powerful (1 Cor. 1:27).

---

12 Langston Hughes, "Mother to Son." Poetry Foundation, http://www.poetryfoundation.org/poem/177021
13 For a potent and clear–eyed look at the disease of consumerism and its pernicious affects on family and community see Affluenza: The All-Consuming Epidemic (Berrett-Koehler Publishers, 2005).

A critical role of the Church in market-driven urban America is to help people take inventory of the talents, treasures, testimonies, and truths that allow them to live lives of decency and dignity, make them producers of culture, and transform them into co-workers in the Kingdom of God. As the elders say, "God don't make no

junk." The restoration of urban America will not take place through gentrification but through "gracification." Only the complete restoration of human dignity of those who are looked upon with contempt can guarantee the healing of the social order. George Fraser once famously that one "who adds value first, wins."[14]

Grace, in this sense, can be conceived of as a participatory encounter when the life that is valuable to God is valuable to human beings. It happens when the Church moves in the power of the Spirit. The Church can both serve and heal the pain of society's victims and advance the reign of God by helping to identify and implement the latent gifts and untapped genius of our embattled neighbors. "Do not forget to show hospitality to strangers," says Hebrews 13:2, "for by so doing some people have shown hospitality to angels without knowing it." These are words that can be used to further god's program.

Radical love compels the Church. It compels us to offer hospitality, because as we invite and nurture strangers, we expand the work of salvation by empowering people to fulfill their God-given purpose. People learn to show radical hospitality based on what is shown to them. Elisha attended to the woman's need; he did not preach a long sermon to her. He did not scold her or shun her for being a welfare recipient. He gave her something invaluable—the gift of time, truth, and a future. Single mothers—like all other children of

---

14 "Fraser Connects the Dots," Black Star News, October 1, 2006. http://www.blackstarnews.com/ny-watch/business/fraser-connects-the-dots.html#sthash.OHwU3vJy.dpuf

God—need to know that the Church can be a place of strengthening and a place of refreshing. How might your Church be this kind of deeply hospitable place for single mothers and other vulnerable people? How might your Church provide support to families of every composition as you welcome them into the family of God?

CHAPTER ELEVEN

SANKOFA:

THE BLESSINGS AND BURDENS OF URBAN EDUCATION IN AMERICA

No pedagogy which is truly liberating can remain distant from the oppressed by treating them as unfortunates and by presenting for their emulation models from among the oppressors. The oppressed must be their own example in the struggle for their redemption.
 —Paolo Friere, Pedagogy of the Oppressed

We cannot have a Lost Generation. If one generation is lost three generations are put at risk. Every generation has the responsibility of taking care of three generations; firstly, itself; secondly, its children; and thirdly, its elders when the infirmities of old age prevent them from taking care of themselves. A lost generation means that one that is unable to take care of themselves, their children or their elders. The reality of this condition has yet to hit us because it is only in middle age that a generation's true nature is found out. "Ye shall know a tree by its fruit," Jesus said. The fruit of a people are its children. The fruit of humanity ripens in middle age when people have reached spiritual, intellectual, emotional and financial maturity. It is at that time when a generation is required to fulfill its threefold task.
 —Clarence Lumumba James, Sr.,
 Lost Generation or Left Generation?

In a global economy where the most valuable skill you can sell is your knowledge, a good education is no longer just a pathway to opportunity—it is a prerequisite. And yet, we have one of the highest high school dropout rates of any industrialized nation. And half of the students who begin college never finish. This is a prescription for economic decline. So tonight, I ask every American to commit to at least one year or more of higher education or career training. This can be community college or a four-year school; vocational training or an apprenticeship. But every American will need to get more than a high school diploma. And dropping out of high school is no longer an option. It's not just quitting on yourself, it's quitting on your country. That's why we will provide the support necessary for all young Americans to complete college and meet a new goal: By 2020, America will once again have the highest proportion of college graduates in the world.

—Barack Obama, 2009 State of the Union Address

THE GREAT DECOY OF EDUCATION[1]

"Urban poor" is a racial code word. It re-presents and replays for the American mind what it most resents about its past and denies about its present. It conjures up images of the unwanted outsider, the permanently damaged person, the social pest. We can hardly overlook the moral weight of this, for in the deep recesses of American cultural memory, urban poor is a "dark" word connoting impurity, ineligibility, and irresponsibility. In an ironic twist, builders and shapers of American cultural lore and language have played with color to enhance America's national identity, beauty, and credibility.[2]

---

1 The title of this section is a spinoff of Stanley Crouch's perceptive look at U.S. race relations, The All-American Skin Game; or, The Decoy of Race (NY: Pantheon Books. 1995).

2 Ralph Ellison and Toni Morrison have shown how America's obsession with whiteness marks almost every area and sector of society, reinforcing a narrow, jingoistic self-understanding, while denigrating people of color. See Toni Morrison's Playing in the Dark: Whiteness and the Literary Imagination (Cambridge: Harvard University Press, 1992) and Ralph Ellison, The Invisible Man (NY: Random House, 1952). In Ellison's grand novel there is a paint-making company called Liberty Paints. Liberty makes white paint by blending an array of colors, many of them darker, one of which is presented as "dead black." In making the final white product the dark

Color, therefore, is a national obsession, an exercise in self-enchantment that serves as a constantly denigrating marker, a totalizing signifier that justifies the institutionalization of our egoistic and exploitative appetites in the name of democracy and civility. Hence, the grammar of color allows America to project onto the world an image of savior and steward, even as it severely circumscribes the gifts and aspirations of those that it punitively labels "less American" or "less human" or some combination of the two. The label, "urban poor," then, is a central marker of America's racial saga. Any attempt to address the plight and predicament of this slice of the population brings to the surface entrenched nativist attitudes that scream fear and loathing. The story of these monumental struggles for selfhood and recognition is what is known as the American experiment.

Urban public education has been prime terrain for this grand historical experiment and thus critical to America's struggle for substantive democracy and racial equality. The most vigorous and imaginative attempts to deconstruct and dismantle America's entrenched social hierarchies have been launched by members of those groups and communities on the underside of mainstream America's bid for supremacy. It is through the public education system that people historically have become "true" Americans, and thus public schools are highly contested and negotiated terrain for the ultimate prize of power, prestige, privilege, and provision. While the primary duties of education are the development of the moral person, the quest for truth, and the cultivation of wisdom (i.e., the development of ethical identity and human communal flourishing), education has functioned in the American context in a more cynical vein: as a passage out of poverty and a passport to power. No other institution presents itself as the key to the ideas,

---

colors dissolve into the mixture, losing their original or distinctive color. The final product is a brilliant sparkling white. As white culture adopts the distinctiveness of different cultures, the other groups lose their distinctiveness. Whiteness is preserved as the universal, regnant, and accepted color of respect and authority.

individuals, and institutions that shape the course and character of society. School is where, for the overwhelming majority of the American people, human destiny is sifted and shaped. Public schools are the womb of the American dream – that ideal of prosperity and possibility that unleashes our egoistic schemes and individualistic wants amidst inexorable fate and circumstance. In our pressurized context of ideological polarization and economic uncertainty, public education is a hit or miss affair of suffocation or salvation. For some it is a world of possibility and life-long opportunity; for others it's a smoldering, life-denying hotbed of repression, coercion, and social isolation.

The American economic structure has always depended on a class of grossly underpaid, largely overworked, and politically disorganized workers. Hence, educational conventions within the American capitalist system seldom develop meaningful innovation that will lead to the restructuring of the American work economy. Moreover, rarely does it generate the creative and constructive forums that can help produce true visionaries who contribute to the creation and sustenance of alternative worlds of justice, equality, and human flourishing.[3] Noble attempts to expand the terrain of true freedom are more often met by retrograde, conservative impulses that reinforce the preexisting social hierarchies based on gender, color, and class. This is done in at least two ways. First, these impulses ensure that forums of "education for competition" outweigh complementary and collaborative forums of "education for liberation."[4] Second, broadly speaking, American education typically elevates the cult of success over the ethic of stewardship. While it is important to develop professional competence and

---

[3] The pervasive dominance of market values consumption more often than not prizes the expert professional over collaboration and teamwork, careerism over vocational responsibility, and academic specialization over intellectual stewardship and partnership.

[4] The two grand examples of this are the social pedagogy of Paulo Freire, Pedagogy of the Oppressed, (New York: Continuum, 1970), and the massive social experiment based on Gandhian nonviolence that supplied the model for the mid-century North American struggle for equality.

technical excellence, a chief aim of education is the reformation of the soul, the repetition of enduring goods, and the institutionalization of intrinsic virtues. Technical efficiency has always served as a lousy substitute for soul formation. One need look no further than Hitler's Germany or Stalin's Russia for grand experiments of technical supremacy and economic efficiency gone bad, the incalculable loss of human life, environmental waste, and social destruction. The U.S. campaign for global domination has left a trail of civic madness and educational mayhem; the urban public schools are left reeling in the wilderness of global capitalism.

While U.S public education is hardly the sole culprit of our cultural malaise, it often functions as fodder for the culture of political domination and economic manipulation that erodes the possibility of unlocking real human potential. Moreover, the political gamesmanship that characterizes many local school boards and state educational committees often reeks of the hardcore ideological tensions that routinely undermine sincere efforts of societal rehabilitation. Regnant pedagogies function as social adjusters to prevailing status quos rather than as developers of whole persons. The larger culture of exploitation thus has a ready supply of captive consumers who are more often than not politically naïve, culturally shallow, and financially strapped. In short, they are bereft of the social capital necessary to mount the kind of organizational crusades necessary for comprehensive social change. The issues around education are infinitely complicated. We must be careful to note that economics alone do not explain the particular character and content of American social tensions. Indeed, there are deeply held fundamentalist worldviews and xenophobic practices that structure and sanction gross systemic inequalities. Endemic white sentiments regarding the innate cultural and intellectual inferiority of the colored citizens of the world simply metastasize within the body politic.[5] Yet the market forces and sensibilities in our world are a chief barrier to the creation of a multi-cultural and multi-ethnic American community.

Urban education addresses poor people and people of color. How they engage education or how education engages them profoundly determines the formation of a national community of substantive democracy. Members of these communities are not mere objects in history, played upon and acted against by persons and procedures not of their own choosing. Rather they are creative subjects, willful contributors to the common good and to the dramas of history. As Ronald Takaki has written in his classic history of a multi-ethnic America, people "have been actors in history, not merely victims of discrimination and exploitation. They are entitled to be viewed as subjects—as men and women with minds, wills and voices."[6] Takaki notes significantly that the stories of these persons are meaningful and "worthy." "Through their stories, the people who have lived [emphasis mine] America's history can help all of us . . . understand that Americans originated from many shores, and that all of us are entitled to dignity."[7] Much of the discourse on education revolves around the need to help marginal communities without paying attention to the rich religious resources, creative visions, emancipatory projects, musical gifts, artistic perspectives, social philosophies, and scientific achievements that members of these communities have brought to the human conversation. This reminds us that the advancement of America as a "free" nation is interwoven with affirmation of the beauty, dignity, and agency of all Americans, since the constitution of the present is the product of a plurality of values, voices, and visions. Since we have all been

---

5 The odyssey of race in America demonstrates that even when whites support mechanisms like affirmative action, they do so because they believe Blacks are inferior.
6 Ronald Takaki, A Different Mirror: A History of Multicultural America, (Boston: Little, Brown and Company, 1993), 15.
7 Takaki, 15-16.

affected by a history of repression and coercion, we all must present ourselves as living sacrifices at the table of rehabilitation. This is the only cure for our addiction to violence, enmity, and strife. The formation of a dynamic theatre of ethnic and cultural pluralism, then, is a chief aim of public education. The global and multicultural American educational system is in need of wholesale revision. Critical to education is cultural retrieval for the sake of moral re-envisioning of our broad and many-faceted past.

Much of the vigorous defense—put forth in the last quarter century—of the western canon (European languages, literature, and logic) as a unified theater of enlightened civilization flattens and conceals the colossal cultural diversity, linguistic heterogeneity, and religious plurality that informs the broad and complex drama that is the very idea of Euro-America itself. Eurocentric and Western-sanctioned multiculturalism is celebrated, defended, and institutionalized as a necessary element of modern human socialization (though in reality Europe itself has in part a blend of older, highly variegated civilizations and cultures). Yet there is a deep suspicion, if not animosity, expressed towards those species of multiculturalism that highlight the visions, contributions, discoveries, literatures, and modes of being from the world of Black, brown, and yellow voices. Modern Christianity itself is guilty of this. It has not always disclosed its own diverse cultural heritage. The classic theological projects of Augustine and Aquinas; the modern democratic visions of philosophers Locke and Jefferson; and the constructive moral formulations of Professors Toni Morrison, Max Stackhouse, Nicholas Wolterstorff, Kosuke Koyama, James Cone, Samuel Escobar, and Mercy Amba Oduyoye have been nourished by intellectual formations linked to highly complex cosmopolitan matrices: Hippo, Jerusalem, Athens, New Haven, Princeton, Lima, Seoul, San Juan, Singapore, Accra, and Ibadan. These thinkers have fused a robust biblical faith with elements of other philo-cultural worldviews as they struggled to come to terms with riddles of existence and the perennial questions of their faith. Moreover, as Virgilio Elizondo has beautifully demonstrated, to cultivate a firmer and clearer picture of the life and teachings of Jesus of Nazareth, it is important to plumb not only the powerful Hebraic spiritual sojourn so wonderfully exemplified in the Law and Prophets, but also the rich and dynamic cultural, linguistic, and social diversity that was Galilee: a hub of imperial power and the site of Jesus' public ministry. The Galilee of Jesus' day was a repository of cultural interchange, cross-ethnic communication, tribal tensions, and religious rivalry.[8] To explore the dramatic life of the Savior is to grapple with the urban roots of Christian mission. Christianity spreads through the tributaries of cross-cultural conversation.

THE STATE OF OUR SCHOOLS

Race and class are defining components of the social fabric of America. Through our attitudes toward certain races and classes, we, the dominant culture, have historically kept outsiders from entering the gate. Hence, mainstream culture has rarely exercised the political will to invest the proper resources and strategies in groups and communities whom we would rather label as inferior, uneducable, uncivilized, and therefore miscreant. People have to be deemed "worthy" in order to get help. Any attempt to understand the American social system cannot overlook this peculiar aspect of its socialization. Yet America has been buttressed by programs that seek to improve the lot of poor and middle-class whites. The American dream, promoted by the Horatio Alger myth, bombards poor people with the attitude that one's will can overcome fate, that we can overcome at any cost. Of course propagandists consistently overlook the barriers of social convention, historical circumstance,

---

[8] During Jesus' lifetime Galilee was peopled by Phoenicians, Syrians, Arabs, Greeks, Asians, and Jews. This may be because Galilee "witnessed multiple invasions by various groups and its geographical setting made it a natural crossing place for international travel routes." Virgilio Elizondo, Galilean Journey: the Mexican-American Promise (Maryknoll, NY: Orbis, 2002), 51.

and political conditions that inscribe the world of the poor, preventing them from emerging from their invisible apartheid. [9]

There is a widespread belief that the educational system functions as a delivery system into the American middle class that will help cure the income inequality gap. Yet according to an article in the Chicago Tribune, many city schools are failing because of the downward spiral in the economy and the lack of quality social amenities that nurture and sustain civil society as a reliable protective canopy for strong families and communities.[10] Many of the schools where the poor attend are themselves inadequately resourced. This means that far too many of our nation's children live in both material poverty and academic poverty. Without an investment in the larger inequalities of the system, the ability of poor children to enter an already unstable and overly competitive work force becomes a mammoth task. The loss of jobs, the recklessness of financial institutions, the rise in cases of mental illness, and the weakening of kinship systems combined with the mushrooming of private consumption, anti-democratic political practices, religious extremism, and hyper-visual and hyper-audio forms of entertainment together have created a dehumanizing wasteland of psychic death.

THE IMPACT OF INADEQUATE EDUCATION

In the eye of this threatening storm are the precious, irreplaceable lives of our children. The repugnant commentary of our age is that

---

[9] The urban institute highlights several factors that delimit the aspirations and abilities of poor children. They include parental income, family structure, family functioning and home environment, and neighborhood factors (e.g., Berger, Paxson, and Waldfogel 2009; Dahl and Lochner 2008; Kling, Lieberman, and Katz 2007; Korenman, Miller, and Sjaastad 1995).Childhood Poverty Persistence: Facts and Consequences. www.urban.org/UploadedPDF/412126-child-poverty-persistence.pdf

[10] Greg J. Duncan and Richard J. Murnane, "Economic Inequality: The Real Cause of the Urban School Problem," Chicago Tribune, October 6, 2011. Critical to this process is the dissemination and celebration that come from these communities and have contributed to the moral and intellectual edification of the human family, along with the intellectual creativity and moral spiritualities that have come from these peoples and the cultural legacies they embody. For this to take place, public education must truly become multi-ethnic and multicultural.

poor children typically go to rundown schools with inadequate facilities where they receive inadequate schooling. They are much less likely than wealthier children to graduate from high school or go to college. Their lack of education in turn restricts them and their own children to poverty, once again helping to ensure a vicious cycle of continuing poverty across generations. As I explained in Chapter 8, "Quilting Hope," scholars debate whether the poor school performance and much of our contemporary woes are rooted in the "might makes right" attitude that pervades corporate America, or whether the problems stem more from the inadequacy of their schools and schooling versus their own poverty. Regardless of exactly why poor children are more likely to do poorly in school and to have low educational attainment, these educational problems are another major consequence of poverty.

According to the National Education Administration, in the year 2000, the high school drop-out rate for Hispanic students was 27.8 percent and the rate for Black students was 13.1 percent. Both of these numbers are significantly higher than the rate of 6.9 percent for white students. "In 2000, young adults living in families with incomes in the lowest 20 percent of all family incomes were six times as likely as their peers from families in the top 20 percent of the income distribution to drop out of high school." The 2009 graduation rate shows an increase of 7.3 percent and includes an increase "for all major racial and ethnic groups, with African-Americans and Latinos showing the most rapid improvements."[11] The high school graduation rate for Philadelphia schools in 2013 was 64 percent. This includes 11 schools with a graduation rate of 90percent or better and 14 schools with a rate of 40 percent or lower. The drop-out rate in Philadelphia for the 2011-2012 year was 6.79 percent (5,986 students).[12]

---

11 "Research Talking Points on Dropout Statistics." http://www.nea.org/home/13579.htm.
12 Dr. Marciene Mattleman, "Philadelphia High School Graduation Rates Up 20 Percent in a Decade," CBS Local, April 15, 2013. http://philadelphia.cbslocal.com/2013/04/15/philadelphia-high-school-graduation-rates-up-20-percent-in-a-decade/

The inevitable consequence of crumbling, ineffectual schools and the poverty surrounding them is that kids leave. They leave when it no longer makes sense to them to stay. A University of Chicago study of education reform summarizes that "schools are complex organizations consisting of multiple interacting subsystems. Each subsystem involves a mix of human and social factors that shape the actual activities that occur and the meaning that individuals attribute to these events. . . In a simple sense, almost everything interacts with everything else."[13] The drop-out rate is tied directly to the unemployment rate. A 2011 Bureau of Labor report indicated high unemployment rates in general during this economy, but the numbers are much worse for the under-educated. The unemployment rate for someone who has not completed high school is 15.4 percent compared to 10 percent for high school graduates and 4.9 percent for those with a bachelor's degree or higher.[14]

SANKOFA: THE MISSION TO RECLAIM OUR CHILDREN

Sankofa is a word from the Akan language of Ghana that means "reach back and get it." It accents the need to recover and reclaim precious realities and foregone possibilities that are central to our identity as a family of God. In the context of urban education it highlights the divine call to heal the faulty education system, combat material poverty, and address the paucity of purpose that characterizes the cities of the most powerful nation in the world. The road to reclaim our cities goes through our young people. An African proverb says, "Children are the reward of life."

---

[13] Anthony S. Bryk et al., Organizing Schools for Improvement: Lessons from Chicago (Chicago: University of Chicago Press, 2010), 46.
[14] Eleni Theodossiou and Steven F. Hipple, "Unemployment Remains High in 2010," Bureau of Labor and Statistics, Monthly Labor Review, March 2011. http://www.bls.gov/opub/mlr/2011/03/art1full.pdf

In *The Scandal of Evangelical Politics,* Ron Sider argues that access to education is a notion parallel to that of the possession of land in the Old Testament: both are the means to an economically secure life. He says, "One of the most important ways to implement the biblical teaching on justice is to offer quality education to all children regardless of race or family income."[15] Children are the co-stewards of our future The Akan of Ghana and Ivory Coast say, "The old woman looks after the child as it grows its teeth and the young one in turn looks after the old woman when she loses her teeth." Christian doctrine arose out of the teaching arm of the Church. The Church has been a place of teaching and learning since its inception (Acts 2:42). Now more than ever we in the Church need to reaffirm and recommit ourselves to the teaching ministry.

The need for such recommitment is especially vital in the urban communities where many are trapped in the economic abyss. Goodmanson reports that in America, 3500 – 4000 Churches close their doors each year. Half of all Churches last year did not add a single new member through conversion growth. Churches lose an estimated 2,765,000 people each year to nominalism and secularism.[16]

Yet urban congregations are not only religious teaching institutions but also "schools" that teach how to negotiate life and understand our culture. How else are we to remain salt and light in the world if we do not know what is happening in the world? The ministry of Jesus reveals His deep immersion in the cultural customs and social habits of the world in which He ministered. The subjects of His parables, His awareness of people's lifestyles, and His method of speaking all reflected His deep understanding of their worlds. Christ became like us. We in turn are called to become like Him.

---

15 Ron Sider, The Scandal of Evangelical Politics (Grand Rapids: Baker Books, 2008), 126.
16 D. Goodmanson, "The Future Dying Church," Sept. 1, 2006. http://www.goodmanson.com/Church/the-future-dying-Church/

The urban Church's commitment to teaching is not only in response to social and spiritual ills; it is quite simply at the heart of discipleship and faith building. In the African American tradition we have mastered the shout and the dance; we have mastered how to preach in such a way that excites the people, but have we done so at the expense of presenting a healthy Gospel and growing people in their faith? With all of our conferences and convocations, has the Church done its due diligence in producing culturally relevant disciples of Christ?

When I first came to my Church, any teaching that was being done outside of Sundays was being done by the diaconate. When I realized that Christian discipleship was not their primary goal, I began to become more hands-on with the teaching responsibilities. I did this until I could put knowledgeable teachers in place that shared my heart and commitment for discipleship.

As part of the Church's responsibility and commissioning to make disciples, the Church teaches people the about the triune God and the historic Christian faith. Most, if not all, Churches have a Christian education ministry responsible for educating believers of all ages. Curricula are in place that educate and instruct parishioners in the faith. The sermons that Black preachers deliver on Sunday mornings are also examples of how they teach and educate their congregations. As it has been since slave days, teaching and education is woven into the very life and liturgy of the Black Church.

As then, so now the Church teaches more than Jesus only. It teaches men and women how to survive in a racialized society: for example, what to do and what not to do when engaged by law enforcement. It teaches congregants how to manage their finances and resources as good stewards so they can provide for their families.

Psalm 25:4 says,

> "Show me your ways, LORD, teach me your paths."

The psalmist asks the Lord to guide and to teach him the path of righteousness. Then as now, God is the divine teacher and we are the students. Just as the twelve disciples had Jesus as their teacher, so now the Spirit guides us into all truth.

Because education is so central to our faith and lives, children and youth ministry is central to re-missioning the Church and our homes. Here are some best practices for re-envisioning urban youth programs in ways that may improve the education of urban children.

- Integrate parents into the system. When parents are part of the process, learning improves dramatically and you create a non-threatening atmosphere that is conducive to learning and the formation of souls.

- Encourage congregation-wide participation in youth ministry and development. Youth ministry is not just for young people but for every believer.

- Reward students and young people for missional work and community service.

- Celebrate and encourage the arts and artists.

- Develop an appreciation for multiple intelligences and learning styles.

- Integrate the sciences through workshops and engineering projects.

- Invest heavily in early childhood development programs that foster not only faith but also a mental fortitude and academic aptitude.

- Remodel and expand Vacation Bible School programs to include field trips, excursions, university visits, travel, sports, mentoring, and coaching life skills.

- Incorporate college prep programs into Christian education and spiritual formation systems.

- Teach on racism, classism, and sexism, and promote cross-cultural experiences.

As a parent of three beautiful children and mentor-father to countless others, I know how crucial education is. Perhaps now more than ever the Church needs to develop programs that help nurture and sustain the frayed bond between families and school systems that exists in urban America.

The Facebook, Twitter, and Instagram generation is now the mission field of the Church. It is a generation unfamiliar with the Church world and language. It is time for us in the Church to exploit social media as a conduit through which to communicate the Gospel. Many in the 40-and-under crowd do not own Bibles and the only exposure to the scriptures they may get is a post on their newsfeed on Facebook. Though social media has the potential to be used for unrighteousness, we can use it to glorify God. The Church does not have to be hesitant to embrace innovative ways to spread the Gospel.

CONCLUSION

TO SERVE THIS PRESENT AGE:
THE CHURCH LIVING IN THE SPIRIT

For all that is flawed in the postmodern, post-Christian world in which we find ourselves, the good news—no, the GREAT NEWS—is that humans once more are seeking the experience of the Divine in our lives.

Throughout this book Scripture has reminded us that no work of lasting significance can be done in the Church without the Spirit. Void of the dynamic, all-encompassing, otherworldly potency of the Spirit, the community of faith forfeits the divine authority and anointing necessary to move the human heart. God never intended for the fallible, fallen human heart to be transformed through finite means. Substantive transformation of head and heart has always been the sole prerogative of the Spirit. The Church is most fully the Church of Jesus Christ when it self-consciously places itself in the power of the Spirit, deriving the full boldness, blessings, and benefits of its fructifying fellowship. According to William MacDonald:

> *This power is the grand indispensable of Christian witness. A man may be highly talented, intensively trained, and widely experienced, but without spiritual power he is ineffective. On the other hand, a man may be uneducated, unattractive, and unrefined, yet let him be endued with the power of the Holy Spirit and the world will turn out to see him burn for God. The fearful disciples needed power for witnessing, holy boldness for preaching the Gospel. They would receive this power when the Holy Spirit came upon them.* [1]

Max Anders reminds us that the Church is not a building. "Unless we see the Church as God sees it, we will be contributing to the problems of Christianity, rather than helping solve them."[2] To see the Church the way God sees it is to assume a posture of creative difference. It is to know that Christ on the cross has cancelled one's sins. This means that one is no longer bound to finite proposals, earthly designs, or worldly ideologies. The winter of mere existence becomes the springtime of passionate commitment, and we see the way of the One who encourages us all—pastors and laypersons alike—to take leaps of faith. There is no need for pastors or leaders to get defensive and protect "their" work or name. Rather, it is the time to be glad that the Spirit frees all believers to engage in apostolic risk taking, to take the leap of faith and reach out to our urban neighbors in need. It is the time to rejoice that because Jesus Christ sent the Spirit to us, we are empowered carry out our mission: to bring hope, help, and healing. This is not ancillary or peripheral to the work of the Church—it is the work of the Church. As Howard Thurman says in his beautiful poem, "The Work of Christmas": "We are to find the lost, to heal the broken, to feed the hungry, to release the prisoner, to rebuild the nations, to bring peace among brothers, to make music in the heart."[3]

---

1 William MacDonald, Believer's Bible Commentary: Old and New Testaments, ed. Arthur Farstad, Ac 1:8 (Nashville: Thomas Nelson, 1995), 1579.
2 Max Anders, What We Need to Know About the Church in 12 Lessons. (Nashville: Thomas Nelson Press, 1997) 24.
3 Howard Thurman, "The Work of Christmas," in The Mood of Christmas and Other Celebrations (Richmond, IN: Friends United Press, 1985), 23.

CONCLUSION

The Church that participates in the life of the Spirit knows that its continued existence depends on these core values. It must evaluate every other preoccupation based on this core set of values and commandments. As the servant Church invites people to be part of its true mission, it brings help, hope, and healing through the Spirit.

EPILOGUE

The Church's theology is only ethically relevant and existentially meaningful within a particular social context. Writing is not the primary form of theology. Rather, theology is "written" in the prayers, preachments, praises, practices, and even prejudices of God's people. It is here that we can witness where the Spirit lives. Yet the search for truth and testimony must also be informed by what the Spirit has to live through. Any theology that does not take a responsible analysis of the social, legal, political, and economic arrangements within a particular context risks being sociologically obsolete. A theology without sociology to guide it becomes arcane and abstract and is of no use to people seeking the existential and spiritual sustenance to cope with the maddened pace of the metropolis. The identity of the missional Church is rooted in fresh understanding of the resurrected Christ. This means that without the person and work of Jesus Christ the Church has no meaning. Christians are to live as disciples in accordance with the teachings and work of Jesus Christ, in the knowledge that He died and was buried, but also in the power of His resurrection and appearance. In word and act we are to serve as Christ on behalf of those members of the population that suffer and are alienated.

In his classic essay "What is the Church?" James Cone states that "the primary definition of the Church is not its confessional affirmation but rather its political commitment on behalf of the poor."[1] How we regard the "least of these" unveils our true intimacy with God and announces to the world how we esteem the life and work of Jesus, the Galilean teacher. Cone asserts that one should never separate the doctrine of the Church from specific local congregations. Rather, theology finds its structure, form, and function when it is concertized within the vitalities of a particular community. Hence, Cone is convinced that it is important to draw a close connection between the theology of the Church and the sociology of the Churches. He states that, "The sociological without the theological reduces the Church to a social club of like-minded people. But the theological without a critical sociological component makes the Church a non-historical, spiritual community, whose existence has no effect on our social and political environment."[2]

This means that one cannot simply highlight the divinity of Christ without acknowledging His exemplary deeds as a human being here on earth. The fact that Jesus healed the wounded, fed the hungry, clothed the naked, and repaired fractured relationships is central to the life of Jesus. And because Jesus is the head of the Church, we are called to embody his teaching and work. Hence, we too must be on the side of those who are exploited and excoriated. Within this framework, Cone challenges Christians of all hues. He believes that if Jesus Christ is the Lord of the Church, as Christians claim, the Church institutions that claim the Christian identity must reflect their commitment to Him in the congregational life of the Church as well as in political and social involvement in society.

My understanding of the role of the Church in the struggle for social equality is informed by the hope that is signified by the awesome, sin-defeating event of resurrection. Christians need to see the

---
[1] James Cone, Speaking the Truth (Grand Rapids: Eerdmans, 1986), 123.
[2] Cone, 115.

resurrection of Jesus Christ as the event that opens up all kinds of possibilities for the human situation in the hands of God who promises to make all things new. Hope, signified and symbolized by the resurrection, gives the poor the energy to combat and change preexisting and dehumanizing social structures. Hence, the present depersonalizing socio-economic arrangements must always be seen as provisional and not permanent. They will be defeated because they are not part of God's ultimate plan for humanity. Human beings can hope for and work towards a society of equality, mutuality, and the opportunity to cultivate moral and creative potentialities. This understanding of hope necessarily highlights the relationship between Christian eschatology and Christian ethics. It is because we expect Jesus Christ to return to fulfill the promise of God that we are to struggle against crisis, corruption, and chaos. This hope is neither escapist nor otherworldly, nor is it solely future-oriented. This is a radical and relentless hope, critically concerned about alienation, discerning about the nature and character of evil in the world, and faithful about the future. Therefore, Christian faith is grounded in the life, death, and resurrection of Jesus Christ.

I believe that I have been called to be a pastor-teacher. Yet my work as a social critic and community organizer has enlivened and energized my pastoral imagination by bringing me into contact with some of America's most gifted, dedicated, and disciplined thinkers. I am privileged to work out of Palmer Theological Seminary, where I am afforded the discursive and dialogic space to grow in a wide array of disciplines and fields. In my opinion the best intellectual conversations take place where you have a multiplicity of voices and a variety of perspectives focused on a common goal or shared interests.

This means that for me scholarship and my Christian development go hand in hand. I praise God through scholarship, I offer thanks through scholarship, and I serve the community through scholarship. I do not believe in acquiring knowledge for its own sake. True community building requires that knowledge be shaped, delineated, defined, reproduced, transformed, and shared. Acquiring knowledge sustains our commitment to a certain goal or body of commitments. And it always involves transformation, criticism, and amendment.

The nature of my vocation has led me to develop certain habits of thought and modes of living that are compatible with the culture of the academy. In particular, I have learned that to be a professor in the Christian tradition and in this age is a difficult and oftentimes overwhelming job. One must try to keep alive a sense of hope that has come under attack both from secular humanists and from pluralistic religionists—not to mention the divisions that are threatening it from within. In addition, one must create a "culture of the soul" that is open to the revelatory activity of the Holy Spirit and the teachings of Jesus Christ. This requires that one open the doors of faith without ignoring the complexities and contingencies of this world. In an increasingly secular and market-driven society, there is the constant temptation to abandon one's purpose for the cultural trappings of the wider secular culture. This is not to say that one's vocation does not extend into the secular or non-Christian world. It simply means that in order to be a Christian and to have a sense of vocation, one's thoughts and actions must be regulated and reformed by non-market values such as care, commitment, and sacrifice, rather than the quest for individualism or the naked search for power, fame, and material gain.

My experience has led me to see the crucial need for training pastors fit for the transformation of society and culture. However, we must be careful not to make this function into a fetish. We must remember that no principality or power can be changed if the souls of human beings are lying fallow across the plains of damnation. As such I want to affirm the two-pronged focus of Jesus' ministry: the healing of the human soul and the overhauling of unjust political regimes.

As such I would like to benefit from both the life of social organizing and social contestation and the culture of the academy. More specifically, I would like to explore what Gardner Taylor calls the "ministry of the word." I want to investigate and illumine the saving activity of Jesus Christ among human beings. This requires a heavy schedule of praying, learning, reading, writing, teaching, and preaching.

These last ten years have instilled in me a deeper commitment to my family, enlarged my moral imagination, expanded my concept of practical Christian theology, and deepened my appreciation for the Bible and the personages to which it gives witness. Thanks be to God!

SELECT BIBLIOGRAPHY

Allen, Ronald J. Preaching the Topical Sermon. Louisville: Westminster/John Knox Press, 1992.

Autry, James A. Love and Profit: The Art of Caring Leadership. New York: Morrow, 1991.

Bannerman, James. The Church of Christ. Birmingham, AL: Solid Ground Christian Books, 2009.

Baxter, Richard. The Reformed Pastor. Edinburgh and Carlisle, PA: Banner of Truth, 1974 [orig.pub. 1656].

Bennett, David W. Metaphors of Ministry. Eugene, OR: Wipf and Stock Publishers, 2004.

Bilezikian, Gilbert. Beyond Sex Roles. Grand Rapids: Zondervan, 1985.

Bilezikian, Gilbert. Community 101. Grand Rapids: Zondervan, 1997.

Blair, Christine Eaton. The Art of Teaching the Bible: A Practical Guide for Adults. Louisville, KY: Geneva Press, 2001.

Bonaventure, Saint. The Character of a Christian Leader (originally titled The Six Wings of the Seraph), trans. Philip O'Mara. Ann Arbor, MI: Servant Books, 1978.

Bonhoeffer, Dietrich. Life Together. New York: Harper and Row, 1954.

Boschman, LaMar. Future Worship. Ventura, CA: Gospel Light Publications, 1999.

Buechner, Frederick. Telling the Truth: The Gospel as Tragedy, Comedy, and Fairy Tale. New York: Harper and Row, 1977.

Carson, D.A. The Cross and Christian Ministry. Grand Rapids: Baker Books, 1993.

Carter, Kenneth H., Jr. The Gifted Pastor: Finding and Using Your Spiritual Gifts. Nashville, TN: Abingdon Press, 2001.

Carter, Rosalynn and Susan Golant. Helping Someone With Mental Illness: A
Compassionate Guide For Family, Friends And Care Givers. New York: Crown Publishing Group, 1998.

Chapell, Bryan. Christ-Centered Preaching. Grand Rapids: Baker Books, 1994.

Clinton, J. Robert. The Making of a Leader. Colorado Springs, CO: NavPress, 1988.

Cone, James. Risks of Faith: The Emergence of a Black Theology of Liberation, 1968–1998. Boston: Beacon Press, 1998.

Conger, Jay A., and Associates. Spirit at Work: Discovering the Spirituality in Leadership. San Francisco: Jossey-Bass Publishers, 1994.

De Pree, Max. Leading Without Power: Finding Hope in Serving Community. San Francisco: Jossey-Bass Publishers, 1997.

Dever, Mark and David Platt. Nine Marks of a Healthy Church. 3rd ed. Wheaton, IL: Crossway, 2013.

Dickson, David. The Elder and His Work. Phillipsburg, NJ: P & R Publishing, 2004.

Fernando, Ajith. Jesus-Driven Ministry. Wheaton, IL: Crossway Books, 2002.

Freedman, Samuel G. Upon This Rock: The Miracles of a Black Church. New York: HarperCollins, 1993.

Gandhi, M. K. Autobiography: The Story of my Experiments with Truth. Washington, D.C.: Public Affairs Press, 1954.

Gandhi, M. K. Non-Violent Resistance (Satyagraha).Mineola, NY: Dover Publications, 2001.

Griffin, Emilie. The Reflective Executive: A Spirituality of Business and Enterprise. New York: Crossroad, 1993.

Harris, Martha L., Diane Engster, and Paul B. Dorman. New Models for Ministry: Serious Mental Illness and the Faith Community. Washington D.C.: New York Ave. Presbyterian Church, 1989.

Harding, Vincent. There is a River: The Black Struggle for Freedom in America. New York: Harcourt Brace Jovanovich, 1981.

Hickman, Craig R., Mind of a Manager, Soul of a Leader. New York: John Wiley &Sons, 1992.

Hughes, R. Kent. Liberating Ministry from the Success Syndrome. Wheaton, IL: Crossway Books, 1987.

Jacobsen, Steve. Hearts to God, Hands to Work: Connecting Spirituality and Work.Bethesda, MD: Alban Institute, 1997 (especially chapter 6).

King, Jr., Martin Luther. Strength to Love. New York: Harper & Row, 1963.

King, Jr., Martin Luther. Stride Toward Freedom. New York: Harper and Row, 1958.

King, Jr., Martin Luther. Where Do We Go From Here? Chaos or Community. New York: Harper & Row, 1967.

Laniak, Timothy. Shepherds After My Own Heart. Downer's Grove, IL: InterVarsity Press, 2006.

Leeman, Jonathan. The Surprising Offense of God's Love. Wheaton, IL: Crossroads Publishing Company, 2010.

Lincoln, C. Eric and Lawrence H. Mamiya. The Black Church in the African American Experience. Durham: Duke University Press, 1990.

Marshall, Colin and Tony Payne. The Trellis and the Vine. Kingsford, NSW: Matthias Media, 2009.

Martin, William C. The Art of Pastoring: Contemplative Reflections. Decatur, GA: CTS Press, 1994.

McClain, Clifford Eugene. Getting Your Own Steeple: A Guide to Pastoral Transition. Kansas City, MO: Jordan Publications, 1986.

Nihinlola, Emiola. "The Weeds Among the Wheat": Hermeneutical Investigation into a Kingdom Parable." Ogbomoso Journal of Theology 12, (January 1, 2007): 87-98.

Nouwen, Henri J.M. In the Name of Jesus: Reflections on Christian Leadership. Wheaton, IL: Crossroads Publishing Company, 1992.

Palmer, Parker J. Leading from Within: Reflections on Spirituality and Leadership. Washington, DC: Potter's House Book Service, 1990 (appears also as chapter 2 in Conger's Spirit at Work: Discovering the Spirituality in Leadership).

Peterson, Eugene H. The Contemplative Pastor: Returning to the Art of Spiritual Direction. Grand Rapids: Eerdmans, 1989.

Peterson, Eugene H. Five Smooth Stones for Pastoral Work. Grand Rapids: Eerdmans, 1980.

Peterson, Eugene H. Under the Unpredictable Plant: An Exploration in Vocational Holiness. Grand Rapids: Eerdmans/Gracewing, 1992.

Peterson, Eugene H., Working the Angles: The Shape of Pastoral Integrity. Grand Rapids: Eerdmans, 1987.

Piper, John. Brothers, We Are Not Professionals. Nashville: B & H Publishing Group, 2013.

Ryken, Philip Graham. City on a Hill. Chicago: Moody, 2003.

Spurgeon, C.H. Lectures to My Students. Grand Rapids: Zondervan, 1954.

Strauch, Alexander. Biblical Eldership. Colorado Springs: Lewis and Roth Publishers, 1995.

Strobel, Shirley H. Creating a Circle Of Learning: The Church and the Mentally Ill. Waldorf, MD: NAMI, 2004.

Waters, Guy Prentiss. How Jesus Runs the Church. Phillipsburg, NJ: P & R Publishing, 2012.

Whyte, David. The Heart Aroused: Poetry and the Preservation of the Soul in Corporate America. New York: Currency Doubleday, 1996.

Witmer, Timothy. The Shepherd Leader. Phillipsburg, NJ: P & R Publishing, 2010.

ABOUT THE AUTHOR

Tokunbo Adelekan is the Senior Pastor of Philadelphia's Mount Olivet Tabernacle Baptist Church. A professor at Eastern University's Palmer Theological Seminary, he works in the areas of theology, ethics, urbanology and post-colonial studies. As a systems organizer, he supports church communities in their efforts to organize around justice and peace issues. His other books include *Leaven in the Loaf: A Comparative Analysis of the Concept of Freedom in the Thought of John Locke and Martin Luther King, Jr.* and *African Wisdom: 101 Proverbs from the Motherland*. He is currently at work on two additional books: *The Arts of the Joseph: The Ministry of Suffering in Vision Formation* and *For Our Transgressions: The Church as a Community of Compassion*.